PAPER
BACK
LYRICS

COMPLETE LYRICS FOR
OVER 125 SONGS

The

2000s

HAL•LEONARD®

ISBN 13: 978-1-4234-1197-0
ISBN 10: 1-4234-1197-8

HAL•LEONARD®
CORPORATION
7777 W. BLUEMOUND RD. P.O. BOX 13819 MILWAUKEE, WI 53213

Visit Hal Leonard Online at
www.halleonard.com

CONTENTS

Accidentally in Love

Words and Music by Adam F. Duritz

from the Motion Picture *Shrek 2*
recorded by Counting Crows

So she said, "What's the problem, baby?"
What's the problem? I don't know.
Well, maybe I'm in love (love).
Think about it, every time I think about it,
Can't stop thinking 'bout it.
How much longer will it take to cure this?
Just to cure it 'cause I can't ignore it
If it's love (love).
Makes me wanna turn around and face me
But I don't know nothing 'bout love. Ah.

Come on, come on, turn a little faster.
Come on, come on, the world will follow after.
Come on, come on, 'cause ev'rybody's after love.

So I said I'm a snowball running,
Running down into the spring that's coming.
All this love melting under blue skies,
Belting out sunlight, shimmering love.
Well, baby, I surrender to the strawberry ice cream,
Never, ever end of all this love.
Well, I didn't mean to do it,
But there's no escaping your love. Ah.
These lines of lightning mean we're never alone,
Never alone, no, no.

Come on, come on, move a little closer.
Come on, come on, I want to hear you whisper.
Come on, come on, settle down inside my love. Ah.

Come on, come on, jump a little higher,
Come on, come on, if you feel a little lighter.
Come on, come on, we were once upon a time in love.

We're accidentally in love, accidentally in love,
Accidentally in love, accidentally in love,
Accidentally in love, accidentally in love,
Accidentally in love, accidentally in love,
Accidentally...

I'm in love, I'm in love, I'm in love,
I'm in love, I'm in love, I'm in love,
Accidentally.

Come on, come on, spin a little tighter.
Come on, come on, and the world's a little brighter.
Come on, come on, just get yourself inside her love.
I'm in love.

All or Nothing

Words and Music by Wayne Hector and Steve Mac

recorded by O-Town

I know when he's been on your mind,
The distant look is in your eyes,
I thought with time you'd realize, it's over, over.
It's not the way I chose to live,
And something somewhere's got to give,
As sharing this relationship gets older, older.
You know I'd fight for you but how can I fight
For someone who isn't even there?
I've had the rest of you, now I want the best of you.
I don't care if that's not fair.

'Cause I want it all, or nothing at all.
There's nowhere left to fall when you reach the bottom;
It's now or never.
Is it all, or are we just friends?
Is this how it ends, with a simple telephone call?
You leave me here with nothing at all.

There are time it seems to me
I'm sharing you with memories.
I feel it in my heart, but I don't show it, show it.
And then there's times you look at me
As though I'm all that you could see.
Those times I don't believe it's right, I know it, know it.
Don't make me promises, baby;
You never did know how to keep them well.
I've had the rest of you, now I want the best of you;
It's time for show and tell.

'Cause I want it all, or nothing at all.
There's nowhere left to fall when you reach the bottom;
It's now or never.
Is it all, or are we just friends?
Is this how it ends, with a simple telephone call?
You leave me here with nothing.

'Cause you and I could lose it all
If you've got no more room,
No room in sight for me in your life.
Cause I want it all, or nothing at all.
There's nowhere left to fall; it's now or never.

Is it all, or nothing at all.
There's nowhere left to fall when you reach the bottom;
It's now or never.
Is it all, or are we just friends?
Is this how it ends, with a simple telephone call?
You leave me here with nothing at all, all.

All the Small Things

Words and Music by Tom De Longe and Mark Hoppus

recorded by Blink 182

All the small things; true care, truth brings.
I'll take one lift. Your ride, best trip.
Always I know, you'll be at my show,
Watching, waiting, commiserating.
Say it ain't so, I will not go,
Turn the lights off, carry me home.

Na na na na na...

Light night, come home.
Work sucks, I know.
She left me roses by the stairs;
Surprises let me know she cares.
Say it ain't so, I will not go,
Turn the lights off, carry me home.

Na na na na na...

Say it ain't so, I will not go,
Turn the lights off, carry me home.
Keep your head still, I'll be your thrill,
The night will go on, my little windmill.

Say it ain't so, I will not go,
Turn the lights off, carry me home.
Keep your head still, I'll be your thrill,
The night will go on, the night will go on,
My little windmill.

Because of You

Words and Music by Kelly Clarkson, Ben Moody and David Hodges

recorded by Kelly Clarkson

I will not make the same mistakes that you did.
I will not let myself cause my heart so much misery.
I will not break the way you did. You fell so hard.
I've learned the hard way to never let it get that far.

Refrain:
Because of you, I never stray too far from the sidewalk.
Because of you, I learned to play on the safe side, so I don't get hurt.
Because of you, I find it hard to trust not only me,
    but everyone around me.
Because of you, I am afraid.

I lose my way, and it's not too long before you point it out.
I cannot cry, because I know that's weakness in your eyes.
I'm forced to fake a smile, a laugh, every day of my life.
My heart can't possibly break when it wasn't even whole to start with.

Refrain

I watched you die; I heard you cry every night in your sleep.
I was so young; you should have known better than to lean on me.
You never thought of anyone else; you just saw your pain,
And now I cry in the middle of the night for the same damn thing.

Because of you, I never stray too far from the sidewalk.
Because of you, I learned to play on the safe side, so I don't get hurt.
Because of you, I try my hardest just to forget everything.
Because of you, I don't know how to let anyone else in.
Because of you, I'm ashamed of my life, because it's empty.
Because of you, I am afraid, because of you, because of you.

Amazed

Words and Music by Marv Green, Chris Lindsey and Aimee Mayo

recorded by Lonestar

Every time our eyes meet,
This feelin' inside me
Is almost more than I can take.
Baby, when you touch me,
I can feel how much you love me,
And it just blows me away.
I've never been this close to anyone or anything.
I can hear your thoughts. I can see your dreams.

Refrain:
I don't know how you do what you do,
I'm so in love with you.
It just keeps gettin' better.
I wanna spend the rest of my life
With you by my side, forever and ever.
Every little thing that you do,
Baby, I'm amazed by you.

The smell of your skin,
The taste of your kiss,
The way you whisper in the dark.
Your hair all around me;
Baby, you surround me.
You touch every place in my heart.
Oh, it feels like the first time every time.
I wanna spend the whole night in your eyes.

Refrain

Every little thing that you do
I'm so in love with you.
It just keeps gettin' better.
I wanna spend the rest of my life
With you by my side forever and ever.
Every little thing that you do,
Oh, every little thing that you do,
Baby, I'm amazed by you.

American Soldier

Words and Music by Toby Keith and Chuck Cannon

recorded by Toby Keith

I'm just tryin' to be a father, raise a daughter and a son.
Be a lover to their mother, everthing to everyone.
Up and at 'em bright and early, I'm all business in my suit.
Yeah, I'm dressed up for success from my head down to my boots.

I don't do it for the money, there's bills that I can't pay.
I don't do it for the glory, I just do it anyway.
Providing for our future's my responsibility.
Yeah, I'm real good under pressure, bein' all that I can be.

And I can't call in sick on Mondays when the weekend's been too strong.
I just work straight through the holidays, sometimes all night long.
You can bet that I stand ready when the wolf growls at the door.
Hey, I'm solid, hey, I'm steady, hey, I'm true down to the core.

And I will always do my duty, no matter what the price.
I've counted up the cost, I know the sacrifice.
Oh, and I don't want to die for you, but if dyin's asked of me,
I'll bear that cross with honor 'cause freedom don't come free.

I'm an American soldier, an American.
Beside my brothers and my sisters I will proudly take a stand.
When liberty's in jeopardy, I will always do what's right.
I'm out here on the front lines, sleep in peace tonight.
American soldier, I'm an American soldier.

Yeah, an American soldier, an American.
Beside my brothers and my sisters I will proudly take a stand.
When liberty's in jeopardy, I will always do what's right.
I'm out here on the front lines, so sleep in peace tonight.
American soldier, I'm an American,
An American, an American soldier.

Are You Gonna Be My Girl

Words and Music by Nic Cester and Cameron Muncey

recorded by Jet

Go!
So one, two, three,
Take my hand and come with me
Because you look so fine
And I really want to make you mine.
I say you look so fine
And I really want to make you mine.

Well, four, five, six,
Come on and get your kicks.
Now you don't need money
When you look like that, do you, honey?
Big black boots, long brown hair.
She's so sweet with her get back stare.

Refrain:
Well I could see you home with me,
But you were with another man, yeah.
I know we ain't got much to say
Before I let you get away, yeah.

Spoken: I said, "Are you gonna be my girl?"

Sung:
Well, it's a one, two, three,
Take my hand and come with me
Because you look so fine
And I really want to make you mine.
I say you look so fine
And I really want to make you mine.

Well, four, five, six,
Come on and get your kicks.
Now you don't need money
With a face like that, do ya?
Big black boots, long brown hair.
She's so sweet with her get back stare.

Refrain

Spoken: I said, "Are you gonna be my girl?"

Refrain

Uh, be my girl. Be my girl.
Are you gonna be my girl? Yeah!

Back Here

Words and Music by Christian Burns, Mark Barry,
    Stephen McNally and Phil Thornalley

recorded by BBMak

Baby, set me free from this misery.
I can't take it no more.
Since you ran away nothin's been the same.
Don't know what I'm livin' for.

Refrain:
Here I am, so alone,
And there's nothing in this world I can do
Until you're back here baby.
Miss you, want you, need you
So until you're back here baby, yeah.
There's a feelin' inside I want you to know.
You are the one and I can't let you go.

So I told you lies, even made you cry.
Baby, I was so wrong.
Girl, I promise you now my love is true.
This is where my heart belongs.

Refrain

And I wonder: Are you thinkin' of me?
'Cause I'm thinkin' of you.
And I wonder: Are you ever comin' back to my life?

Here I am, so alone,
And there's nothing in this world I can do
Until you're back here baby.
Miss you, want you, need you
So until you're back here baby, yeah.
There's a feelin' inside I want you to know.

You are the one and I can't
Until you're back here baby.
Until you're back here baby.
Until you're back here baby.
There's a feelin' inside I want you to know.
You are the one and I can't
Until you're back here baby.

Repeat and Fade:
Until you're back here baby.

Be Yourself

Lyrics by Chris Cornell
Music written and arranged by Audioslave

recorded by Audioslave

Someone falls to pieces sleeping all alone.
Someone kills the pain.
Spinning in the silence, she finally drifts away.
Someone gets excited in a chapel yard
And catches a bouquet.
Another lays a dozen white roses on a grave.

Yeah, and to be yourself is all that you can do, yeah.
To be yourself is that you can do, oh.

Someone finds salvation in everyone,
Another lonely pain.
Someone tries to hide himself, down inside himself he prays.
Someone swears his true love until the end of time,
Another runs away.
Separate or united, healthy or insane.

And to be yourself is all that you can do, yeah.
(All that you can do.)
To be yourself is all that you can do.
(All that you can do.)
To be yourself is all that you can do, ay.
(All that you can do.)
Be yourself is all that you can do.

Even when you've paid enough, been put upon,
Or been held up with every single memory
Of the good or bad faces of luck.
Don't lose any sleep tonight
I'm sure everything will end up alright.

You may win or lose but
To be yourself is all that you can do, yeah.
To be yourself is all that you can do, oh.
To be yourself is all that you can do, yeah.
(All that you can do.)
To be yourself is all that you can do, yeah.
(All that you can do.)
To be yourself is all that you can,
Be yourself is all that you can,
Be yourself is all that you can do.

Beautiful

Words and Music by Linda Perry

recorded by Christina Aguilera

Every day is so wonderful,
Then suddenly, it's hard to breathe.
Now and then I get insecure from all the pain,
Feel so ashamed.

I am beautiful no matter what they say.
Words can't bring me down.
I am beautiful in every single way.
Yes, words can't bring me down, oh no.
So don't you bring me down today.

To all your friends you're delirious.
So consumed in all your doom.
Trying hard to fill the emptiness.
The pieces gone, left the puzzle undone.
Ain't that the away it is?

You are beautiful no matter what they say.
Words can't bring you down.
You are beautiful in every single way.
Yes, words can't bring you down, oh no.
So don't you bring me down today.

No matter what we do. No matter what we say.
We're the song inside the tune full of beautiful mistakes.
And everywhere we go the sun will always shine.
And tomorrow we might awake on the other side.
'Cause we are beautiful no matter what they say.
Words can't bring us down.
We are beautiful in every single way.
Yes, words won't bring us down, oh no.
So don't you bring me down today.

Don't you bring me down today, yeah, ooh.
Don't you bring me down um today.

Beautiful Soul

Words and Music by Andy Dodd and Adam Watts

recorded by Jesse McCartney

Refrain:
I don't want another pretty face.
I don't want just anyone to hold.
I don't want my love to go to waste.
I want you and your beautiful soul.

I know that you are something special.
To you I'd be always faithful.
I want to be what you always needed.
Then I hope you'll see the heart in me.

Refrain

You're the one I want to chase.
You're the one I want to hold.
I won't let another minute go to waste.
I want you and your beautiful soul.

Your beautiful soul, yeah.

You might need time to think it over.
But I'm just fine moving forward.
I'll ease your mind if you give me the chance.
I will never make you cry. C'mon let's try.

Refrain

Am I crazy for wantin' you?
Baby, do you think you could want me too?
I don't wanna waste your time.
Do you see things the way I do?
I just want to know that you feel it too.
There is nothing left to hide.

I don't want another pretty face.
I don't want just anyone to hold.
I don't want my love to go to waste.
I want you and your soul.

I don't want another pretty face.
I don't want just anyone to hold.
I don't want my love to go to waste.
I want you and your beautiful soul, oh.
Your beautiful soul, yeah.

Beer for My Horses

Words and Music by Toby Keith and Scott Emerick

recorded by Toby Keith

Well, a man come on the six o'clock news,
Said somebody's been shot, somebody's been abused.
Somebody blew up a building, somebody stole a car,
Somebody got away, somebody didn't get too far, yeah.
They didn't get too far.

Grandpappy told my pappy, back in my day, son,
A man had to answer for the wicked that he done.
Take all the rope in Texas, find a tall oak tree,
Round up all of them bad boys, hang 'em high in the street
For all the people to see that

Refrain:
Justice is the one thing you should always find.
You got to saddle up your boys, you got to draw a hard line.
When the gun smoke settles, we'll sing a victory tune.
We'll all meet back at the local saloon.
We'll raise up our glasses against evil forces, singing,
"Whiskey for my men, beer for my horses."

We got too many gangsters doing dirty deeds.
We've got too much corruption, too much crime in the streets.
It's time the long arm of the law put a few more in the ground,
Send 'em all to their Maker and He'll settle 'em down.
You can be He'll settle 'em down, 'cause

Refrain

"Whiskey for my men, beer for my horses."

Refrain

Singing, "Whiskey for my men, beer for my horses."

Believe

Words and Music by Glen Ballard and Alan Silvestri

from Warner Bros. Pictures' *The Polar Express*
recorded by Josh Groban

Children sleeping, snow is softly falling.
Dreams are calling like bells in the distance.
We were dreamers, not so long ago,
But one by one, we all had to grow up.
When it seems the magic slipped away,
We find it all again on Christmas Day.

Refrain:
Believe in what your heart is saying,
Hear the melody that's playing.
There's no time to waste, there's so much to celebrate.
Believe in what you feel inside
And give your dreams the wings to fly.
You have everything you need if you just believe.

Trains move quickly to their journey's end.
Destinations are where we begin again.
Ships go sailing far across the sea,
Trusting starlight to get where they need to be.
When it seems that we have lost our way,
We find ourselves again on Christmas Day.

Refrain

If you just believe, if you just believe.
If you just believe.
Just believe, just believe.

Bless the Broken Road

Words and Music by Marcus Hummon, Bobby Boyd and Jeff Hanna

recorded by Rascal Flatts

I set out on a narrow way many years ago,
Hoping I would find true love along the broken road.
But I got lost a time or two,
Wiped my brow and kept pushin' through.
I couldn't see how every sign pointed straight to you.

But every long lost dream led me to where you are.
Others who broke my heart, they were like northern stars
Pointing me on my way into your loving arms.
This much I know is true: that God blessed the broken road
That led me straight to you. Yes, He did.

I think about the years I've spent just passin' through.
I'd like to have the time I lost and give it back to you.
But you just smile and take my hand.
You've been there, you understand
It's all part of a grander plan that is comin' true.

Every long lost dream led me to where you are.
Others who broke my heart, they were like northern stars
Pointing me on my way into your loving arms.
This much I know is true: that God blessed the broken road
That led me straight to you.

Now I'm just a rollin' home into my lover's arms.
This much I know is true: that God blessed the broken road
That led me straight to you,
That God blessed the broken road that led me straight to you.

Best of You

Words and Music by Dave Grohl, Taylor Hawkins, Chris Shiflett and Nate Mendel

recorded by Foo Fighters

I've got another confession to make: I'm your fool.
Everyone's got their chains to break holding you.
Were you born to resist, or be abused?

Is someone getting the best,
The best, the best, the best of you?
Is someone getting the best,
The best, the best, the best of you?
Are you gone and on to someone new?

I needed somewhere to hang my head without your noose.
You gave me something that I didn't have, but had no use.
I was too weak to give in, too strong to lose.

My heart is under arrest again, but I break loose.
My head is giving me life or death, but I can't choose.
I swear I'll never give in, I refuse.

Is someone getting the best,
The best, the best, the best of you?
Is someone getting the best,
The best, the best, the best of you?

Has someone taken your faith?
It's real, the pain you feel.
Your trust, you must confess.
I someone getting the best,
The best, the best, the best of you?
Oh. Oh, oh, oh, oh.

Has someone taken your faith?
It's real, the pain you feel.
The life, the love you thought you healed.
The hope that stops the broken hearts.
Your trust, you must confess.

Is someone getting the best,
The best, the best, the best of you?
Is someone getting the best,
The best, the best, the best of you?

I've got another confession my friend: I'm no fool.
I'm getting' tired of starting again somewhere new.
Were you born to resist or be abused?
I swear I'll never give in, I refuse.

Is someone getting the best,
The best, the best, the best of you?
Is someone getting the best,
The best, the best, the best of you?

Has someone taken your faith?
It's real, the pain you feel.
Your trust, you must confess.
Is someone getting the best,
The best, the best, the best of you?
Oh.

Beverly Hills

Words and Music by Rivers Cuomo

recorded by Weezer

Where I come from isn't all that great.
My automobile is a piece of crap.
My fashion sense is a little whack
And my friends are just as screwy as me.
I didn't go to boarding schools,
Preppy girls never looked at me.
Why should they?
I ain't nobody, got nothin' in my pocket.

Beverly Hills, that's where I want to be.
(Gimmie, gimmie, gimmie, gimmie.)
Living in Beverly Hills.
Beverly Hills, rollin' like a celebrity.
Living in Beverly Hills.

Look at all those movie stars,
They'are all so beautiful and clean.
When the housemaids scrub the floors
They get the spaces in between.
I wanna live a life like that. I wanna be just like a king.
Take my picture by the pool 'cause I'm the next big thing in…

Beverly Hills, that's where I want to be.
(Gimmie, gimmie, gimmie, gimmie.)
Living in Beverly Hills.

Spoken:
The truth is, I don't stand a chance.
It's something that you're born into and I just don't belong.

Sung:
No I don't, I'm just a no-class, beat down fool
And I will always be that way.
I might as well enjoy my life and watch the stars play.

Beverly Hills, that's where I want to be.
(Gimmie, gimmie, gimmie, gimmie.)
Living in Beverly Hills.
Beverly Hills, Beverly Hills. Yeah!
Beverly Hills, Beverly Hills.
Living in Beverly Hills.

Blessed

Words and Music by Brett James, Hillary Lindsey and Troy Verges

recorded by Martina McBride

I get kissed by the sun each morning,
Put my feet on a hardwood floor.
I get to hear my children laughing
Down the hall through the bedroom door.

Sometimes I sit on my front porch swing,
Just soakin' up the day.
I think to myself, I think to myself
This world is a beautiful place.

Refrain:
I have been blessed.
And I feel like I found my way.
I thank God for all I've been given
At the end of every day.
I have been blessed
With so much more than I deserve,
To be here with the ones who love me,
To love them so much it hurts.
I have been blessed.

Across the crowded room
I know you know what I'm thinkin'
By the way I look at you.
And when we're lying in the quiet
And no words have to be said,
I think to myself, I think to myself,
"This love is a beautiful gift."

Refrain

When I, when I'm, singin' my kids to sleep,
When I feel you holdin' me, I know I am so blessed.
And I feel like I found my way.
I thank God for all I've been given
At the end of every day.
I have been blessed with so much more than I deserve,
To be here with the ones who love me,
To love them so much it hurts.
I have been blessed.
Oh, yes, I have been blessed,
Oh, yeah, yeah.

Repeat and Fade:
I have been blessed, I have been blessed.

Breakaway

Words and Music by Bridget Benenate, Avril Lavigne and Matthew Gerrard

from *The Princess Diaries 2: Royal Engagement*
recorded by Kelly Clarkson

Dah, dah, dah, dah, dah…

Grew up in a small town
And when the rain would fall down,
I'd just stare out my window.
Dreamin' of what could be
And if I'd end up happy.
I would pray.

Trying hard to reach out
But when I tried to speak out,
Felt like no one could hear me.
Wanted to belong here
But something felt so wrong here.
So I'd pray. (I would pray)
I could breakaway.

Refrain:
I'll spread my wings and I'll learn how to fly.
I'll do what it takes 'til I touch the sky.
I'll make a wish. Take a chance.
Make a change and breakaway.

Out of the darkness and into the sun.
But I won't forget all the ones that I love.
I'll take a risk. Take a chance.
Make a change and breakaway.

Dah, dah, dah, dah, dah...

Wanna feel the warm breeze.
Sleep under a palm tree.
Feel the rush of the ocean.
Get on board a fast train.
Travel on a jet plane far away and breakaway.

Refrain

Out of the darkness and into the sun.
But I won't forget all the ones that I love.
I gotta take a risk. Take a chance.
Make a change and breakaway.

Building with a hundred floors.
Swinging 'round revolving doors.
Maybe I don't know where they'll take me.
But, gotta keep movin' on, movin' on.
Fly away, breakaway.

I'll spread my wings and I'll learn how to fly.
Though it's not easy to tell you goodbye,
Gotta take a risk. Take a chance.
Make a change and breakaway.

Out of the darkness and into the sun.
But I won't forget the place I come from.
I gotta take a risk. Take a chance.
Make a change and breakaway,
Breakaway, breakaway.

Breathe

Words and Music by Holly Lamar and Stephanie Bentley

recorded by Faith Hill

I can feel the magic floating in the air.
Being with you gets me that way.
I watch the sunlight dance across your face
And I've never been this swept away.

All my thoughts just seem to settle on the breeze,
When I'm lyin' wrapped up in your arms.
The whole world just fades away,
The only thing I hear is the beating of your heart.

Refrain:
'Cause I can feel you breathe,
It's washing over me,
And suddenly I'm melting into you.
There's nothing left to prove,
Baby, all we need is just to be
Caught up in the touch,
The slow and steady rush.
Baby, isn't that the way
That love's supposed to be?
I can feel you breathe.
Just breathe.

In a way I know my heart is wakin' up
As all the walls come tumbling down.
Closer than I've ever felt before,
And I know and you know
There's no need for words right now.

Refrain

Caught up in the touch,
The slow and steady rush.
Baby, isn't that the way
That love's supposed to be?
I can feel you breathe.
Just breathe.
I can feel the magic floating in the air.
Bein' with you gets me that way.

Burn

Words and Music by Usher Raymond, Jermaine Dupri and Bryan Michael Cox

recorded by Usher

Spoken:
I don't understand why.
See it's burnin' me to hold on to this
I know this is somethin' I gotta do.
But that don't mean I want to.
What I'm tryin' to say is that I love you.
I just, I feel like this is comin' to an end.
And it's better for me to let it go now
Than to hold on and hurt you.
I gotta let it burn.

Sung:
It's gon' burn for me to say this.
It's comin' from my heart.
It's been a long time comin'
But we done been fell apart.
I really want to work this out
But I don't think you're gonna change.
I do but you don't think it's best we go our separate ways.
Tell me why I should stay in this relationship
When I'm hurtin' baby? I ain't happy baby.
Plus there's so many other things I gotta deal with.
I think that you should let it burn.

Refrain:
When the feelin' ain't the same in your body.
Don't want to, but you know, got to let it go
'Cause the party ain't jumpin' like it used to.
Even though this might bruise you.
Let it burn. Gotta let it burn.

Deep down you know it's best for you
'Cept but you hate the thought of her
Being with someone else.
But you know that it's over.
You know'd it was through.
Let it burn, let it burn. Gotta let it burn.

Sendin' pages I ain't s'posed to.
Got somebody here but I want you.
'Cause the feelin' ain't the same.
Find myself calling her your name.
Ladies tell me do you understand?
Now, all my fellas, do you feel my pain?
It's the way I feel. I knew I made a mistake.
Now it's too late. I know she ain't comin' back.
What I gotta do now to get my shorty back?
Ooh, ooh, ooh, ooh,
Man, I don't know what I'm gonna do without my boo.
You've been gone for too long.
It's been fifty 'leven days, umteen hours.
I'm-a be burnin' till you return.

Refrain

I'm twisted 'cause one side of me's
Tellin' me that I need to move on.
On the other side I wanna break down and cry.
Ooh, I'm twisted 'cause one side of me's
Tellin' me that I need to move on.
On the other side I wanna break down and cry, yeah.
Ooh, ooh, ooh, ooh, ooh, ooh.
Ooh, ooh, ooh, can you feel me burnin'?
Ooh, ooh, ooh, ooh, ooh, ooh.
So many days, so many hours.
I'm still burnin' till you return.

Refrain

By the Way

Words and Music by Anthony Kiedis, Flea, John Frusciante and Chad Smith

recorded by Red Hot Chili Peppers

Standing in line to see the show tonight
And there's a light on, heavy glow.
By the way I tried to say I'd be there
Waiting for Dani, the girl that's singing songs to me
Beneath the marquee, overlaod.

Steak knife. Card shark. Con job. Boot cut.
Spoken: Skin that flick, she's such a little B.J.
Get there quick by street but not by freeway.
Turn that trick to make a little leeway.
Beat that meat but not the way that we play.

Sung:
Dog town. Bloodbath. Ribcage. Soft tail.
Standing in line to see the show tonight
And there's a light on, heavy glow.
By the way I tried to say I'd be there waiting for.

Blackjack. Dope dick. Pawn shop. Quick pick.
Spoken: Kiss that dyke, I know you want to hold one.
Not on strike but I'm about to bowl one.
Bite that mic, I know you never stole one.
Girls that like a story so I told one.

Sung:
Song bird. Main line. Cash back. Hard top.
Standing in line to see the show tonight
And there's a light on, heavy glow.
By the way I tried to say I'd be there
Waiting for Dani the girl that's singing songs to me
Beneath the marquee, oversold.
By the way I tried to say I'd be there waiting for.

Spoken:
Ooh, aah, kiss ya then I miss ya.
Ooh, aah, kiss ya then I miss ya.
Ooh, aah, kiss ya then I miss ya.
Ooh, aah, kiss ya then I miss ya.
Ooh, aah, kiss ya then I miss ya.
Ooh, aah, kiss ya then I miss ya.
Ooh, aah, kiss ya then I miss ya.
Ooh, aah.

Sung:
Standing in line to see the show tonight
And there's a light on, heavy glow.
By the way I tried to say I'd be there
Waiting for Dani, the girl that's singing songs to me
Beneath the marquee, oversold.
By the way I tried to say I know you from before.

Standing in line to see the show tonight
And there's a light on, heavy glow.
By the way I tried to say I'd be there waiting for.

By Your Side

Words by Sade Adu
Music by Sade Adu, Stuart Matthewman, Andrew Hale and Paul Spencer Denman

recorded by Sade

You think I'd leave your side, baby?
You know me better than that.
Think I'd leave you down
When you're down on your knees?
I wouldn't do that.
I'll tell you you're right when you want.
Ha, ha, ha, ha, ha, mm.
If only you could see into me.

Oh, when you're cold, I'll be there.
Hold you tight to me.
When you're on the outside, baby,
And you can't get in, I will show you
You're so much better than you know.

When you're lost and you're alone,
And you can't get back again,
I will find you, darling, and I'll bring you home.
And if you want to cry, I am here to dry your eyes.
And in no time you'll be fine.

You think I'd leave your side, baby?
You know me better than that.
Think I'd leave you down
When you're down on your knees?
I wouldn't do that.
I'll tell you you're right when you want.
Ha, ha, ha, ha, ha, mm.
If only you could see into me.

Oh, when you're cold, I'll be there.
Hold you tight to me.
Oh, when you're low, I'll be there
By your side, baby.

Calling All Angels

Words and Music by Pat Monahan, Scott Underwood,
  James Stafford and Charlie Colin

recorded by Train

I need a sign to let me know you're here.
All of these lines are being crossed over the atmosphere.
I need to know that things are gonna look up
'Cause I feel us drowning in a sea spilled from a cup.
When there is no place safe and no safe place to put my head.
When you can feel the world shake from the words that are said.
And I'm calling all angels. And I'm calling all you angels.

And I won't give up if you don't give up.
I won't give up if you don't give up.
I won't give up if you don't give up.
I won't give up if you don't give up.

I need a sign to let me know you're here
'Cause my T.V. set just keeps it all from being clear.
I want a reason for the way things have to be.
I need a hand to help build up some kind of hope inside of me.
And I'm calling all angels. And I'm calling all you angels.

When children have to play inside so they don't disappear,
While private eyes solve marriage lies 'cause we don't talk for years.
And football teams are kissing queens and losing sight of having dreams
In a world where what we want is only what we want until it's ours.
And I'm calling all angels. And I'm calling all you angels.

And I'm (I won't give up if you don't give up.)
Calling all angels. (I won't give up if you don't give up.)
And I'm (I won't give up if you don't give up.)
Calling all you angels. (I won't give up if you don't give up.)

Repeat and Fade:
Calling all you angels. (I won't give up if you don't give up.)
Calling all you angels. (I won't give up if you don't give up.)

Can't Get You Out of My Head

Words and Music by Cathy Dennis and Rob Davis

recorded by Kylie Minogue

La, la, la, la…

Refrain:
I just can't get you out of my head.
Boy, your lovin' is all I think about.
I just can't get you out of my head.
Boy, it's more than I dare to think about.

La, la, la, la…

Refrain

Every night, every day.
Just to be there in your arms.
Won't you stay?
Won't you lay with me forever,
And ever, and ever, and ever?

La, la, la, la…

Refrain

There's a dark secret in me.
Don't leave me locked in your heart.
Set me free. Feel the need in me.
Set me free. With me forever,
And ever, and ever, and ever.

La, la, la, la...

Repeat and Fade:
I just can't get you out of my head,
La, la, la, la...

Case of the Ex (Whatcha Gonna Do)

Words and Music by Christopher Stewart, Traci Hale and Thabiso Nkhereanye

recorded by Mya

It's after midnight and she's on your phone.
She's saying come over, 'cause she's all alone.
I could tell it was your ex by your tone,
So why is she calling now, after so long?
Now, what is it that she wants?
Tell me, what is it that she needs?
Did she hear about the brand new Benz
That you just bought for me?
'Cause y'all didn't have no kids,
Didn't share no mutual friends,
And you told me that she turned trick
When y'all broke up in ninety-six.

Refrain (Six Times):
What you gon' do when you can't say no
And her feelings start to show?
Boy, I really need to know, and how you gonna act?
How you gonna handle that?
What you gon' do when she wants you back?

Tell me, why she on the phone in the middle of the night?
Tell me, why she in your life tryin' to get what's mine?
She don't know me; she's about to know me.
I'm in your life, that's how it's gon' be.
I've seen her photo; she ain't even all that,
So if you want her back you can take her back,
'Cause game recognize game. I can do the same thing.
Get it right; change, or take back this ring.

Refrain Four Times

Clint Eastwood

Words and Music by 2D, Murdoc Niccals and Teren Delvon Jones

recorded by Gorillaz

Refrain:
I ain't happy, I'm feeling glad.
I got sunshine in a bag.
I'm useless, but not for long.
The future is coming on.
I ain't happy, I'm feeling glad.
I got sunshine in a bag.
I'm useless, but not for long.
The future is coming on,
Is coming on, is coming on,
Is coming on, is coming on, is...

Rap:
Finally someone let me out of my cage.
Now time for me is nothing, 'cause I'm counting no age.
Nah, I couldn't be there. Nah, you shouldn't be scared.
I'm good at repairs and I'm under each snare.
Intangible. Bet you didn't think so, I command you to.
Panoramic view, look, I'll make it all manageable.
Pick and choose, sit and lose, all you different crews.
Chicks and dudes, who you think is really kicking tunes?
Picture you getting down in a picture tube,
Like you lit the fuse. You think it's fictional? Mystical?
Maybe spiritual? Hero who appears in you to clear your view
When you're too crazy.

Lifeless. To know the definition for what life is.
Priceless for you, because I put you on the hype shit.
You like it? Gun smoking righteous with one token psychic
Among those possess you with one go.

Refrain

Rap:
The essence, the basics, without it you make it.
Allow me to make this childlike in nature.
Rhythm, you have it or you don't, that's a fallacy.
I'm in them, every sprouting tree, every child apiece,
Every cloud and sea. You see with your eyes,
I see destruction and demise, corruption in disguise
From this fucking enterprise. Now I'm sucked into your lies.
Through Russ, though not his muscles, but percussion he provides
With me as a guide. Y'all can see me now,
'Cause you don't see with your eye, you perceive with your mind.
That's the end, hon. So I'm a stick around with Russ and be a mentor.
But a few rhymes, so motherfuckers remember
Where the thought is. I brought all this so you can survive
When law is lawless.
Feelings, sensations that you thought was dead,
No squealing, remember that it's all in your head.

Refrain

My future is coming on, is coming on, is coming on.
My future is coming on, is coming on, is coming on.
My future.

Clocks

Words and Music by Guy Berryman, Jon Buckland, Will Champion and Chris Martin

recorded by Coldplay

Lights go out and I can't be saved.
Tides that I tried to swim against
Brought me down upon my knees.
Oh, I beg, I beg and plead.
Singin', come out of things unsaid.
Shoot an apple off my head.
And a trouble that can't be named.
A tiger's waiting to be tamed.
Singin', you are. You are.

Confusion never stops.
Closing walls and ticking clocks
Gonna come back and take you home.
I could not stop that you now know.
Singin', come out upon my seas,
Curse missed opportunities.
Am I a part of the cure
Or am I part of the disease?
Singin', you are. You are.

You are. You are.
You are. You are.
And nothing else compares.

You are. You are.
You are. You are.
Home, home, where I wanted to go.
Home, home, where I wanted to go.
Home, home, where I wanted to go.
Home, home, where I wanted to go.

Come a Little Closer

Words and Music by Dierks Bentley and Brett Beavers

recorded by Dierks Bentley

Come a little closer, baby,
I feel like layin' you down
On a bed of sweet surrender,
Where we can work it all out.

Thre ain't nothin' that love can't fix.
Girl, it's right here at our fingertips.
So, come a little closer, baby,
I feel like layin' you down.

Come a little closer, baby, I feel like lettin' go
Of everything that stands between us
And the love we used to know.
I wanna touch you like a cleansing rain
And let it wash all the hurt away.
So, come a little closer, baby, I feel like lettin' go.

If there's still a chance,
Then take my hand and we'll steal away
Off into the night till we make things right.
The sun's gonna rise on a better day.

Come a little closer, baby, I feel like strippin' it down.
Back to the basics of you and me
And what makes the world go 'round.
Every inch of you against my skin,
I wanna be stronger than we've ever been.
So, come a little closer, baby, I feel like strippin' it down.

Come a little closer, baby, just a little bit closer, baby.
Come a little closer, baby, I feel like layin' you down.

Complicated

Words and Music by Avril Lavigne, Lauren Christy, Scott Spock and Graham Edwards

recorded by Avril Lavigne

Spoken:
Uh huh, life's like this.
Uh huh, uh huh, that's the way it is.
'Cause life's like this.
Uh huh, uh huh, that's the way it is.

Sung:
Chill out, whatcha yellin' for?
Lay back, it's all been done before.
And if you could only let it be you will see.
I like you the way you are
When we're drivin' in tour car
And you're talkin' too me
One on one but you become

Somebody else 'round everyone else.
You're watching your back like you can't relax.
You're tryin' to be cool.
You look like a fool to me.

Tell me, why'd you have to go
And make things so complicated?
See the way you're acting
Like you're somebody else, gets me frustrated.
Life's like this, you, you fall and you crawl
And you break and you take what you get
And you turn it into honesty and promise me
I'm never gonna find you fake it, no, no, no.

You came over unannounced,
Dressed up like you're something else.
Where you are ain't where it's at, you see.
You're makin' me laugh out when you strike your pose.
Take off all your preppy clothes.
You know you're not foolin' anyone when you become

Somebody else 'round everyone else.
You're watching your back like you can't relax.
You're tryin' to be cool.
You look like a fool to me.

Tell me, why'd you have to go
And make things so complicated?
See the way you're acting
Like you're somebody else, gets me frustrated.
Life's like this, you, you fall and you crawl
And you break and you take what you get
And you turn it into honesty and promise me
I'm never gonna find you fake it, no, no, no, no,
No, no, no, no, no, no, no, no, no, no, no, no.
Chill out, whatcha yellin' for?

Lay back, it's all been done before.
And if you could only let it be you will see
Somebody else 'round everyone else.
You're watching your back like you can't relax.
You're tryin' to be cool.
You look like a fool to me.

Tell me, why'd you have to go
And make things so complicated?
See the way you're acting
Like you're somebody else, gets me frustrated.
Life's like this, you, you fall and you crawl
And you break and you take what you get
And you turn it into honesty. Promise me
I'm never gonna find you fake it, no, no,

Why'd you have to go
And make things so complicated?
See the way you're acting
Like you're somebody else, gets me frustrated.
Life's like this, you, you fall and you crawl
And you break and you take what you get
And you turn it into honesty and promise me
I'm never gonna find you fake it, no, no, no.

The Cowboy in Me

Words and Music by Craig Wiseman, Alan Anderson and Jeffrey Steele

recorded by Tim McGraw

I don't know why I act the way I do,
Like I ain't got a single thing to lose.
Sometimes I'm my own worst enemy.
I guess that's just the cowboy in me.

I got a life that most would love to have.
But sometimes I still wake up fightin' mad
At where this road I'm headin' down might lead.
I guess that's just the cowboy in me.

Refrain (Sing Twice):
The urge to run, the restlessness,
The heart of stone I sometimes get.
The things I've done for foolish pride,
The me that's never satisfied.
The face that's in the mirror
When I don't like what I see.
I guess that's just the cowboy in me.

Girl, I know there's time you must have thought
There ain't a line you've drawn I haven't crossed.
But you set your mind to see this love on through.
I guess that's just the cowboy in you.

We ride and never worry 'bout the fall.
I guess that's just the cowboy in us all.

Crazy in Love

Words and Music by Rich Harrison, Shawn Carter and Beyonce Knowles

recorded by Beyonce featuring Jay-Z

Spoken:
Male: Yes, it's so crazy right now.
Most incredibly, it's your girl B. It's your boy young.
Female: You ready?

Sung:
Uh-oh, uh-oh, oh, oh, no, no.
Uh-oh, uh-oh, oh, oh, no, no.
Uh-oh, uh-oh, oh, oh, no, no.
Uh-oh, uh-oh, oh, oh, no, no.

Spoken:
History in the making part two.
It's so crazy right now.

I love to stare so deep in your eyes.
I touch on you more and more every time.
When you leave, I'm beggin' you not to go.
Call your name two or three times in a row.
Such a funny thing for me to try to explain,
How I'm feelin' and my pride is the one to blame.
'Cause I know I don't understand just how
Your love can do what no one else can.

Refrain:
Got me lookin' so crazy right now,
Your love's got me lookin' so crazy right now.
Your love got me lookin' so crazy right now.
Your touch got me lookin so crazy right now.
Your touch got me hopin' you'll page me right now.
Your kiss got me hopin' you'll save me right now.
Lookin' so crazy, your love's got me lookin',
Got me lookin' so crazy in love.

Uh-oh, uh-oh, oh, oh, no, no.
Uh-oh, uh-oh, oh, oh, no, no.
Uh-oh, uh-oh, oh, oh, no, no.
Uh-oh, uh-oh, oh, oh, no, no.

When I talk to my friends so quietly,
Look at what you did to me.
Tennis shoes, don't even need to buy a new dress.
If you ain't there, ain't nobody else to impress.
It's just the way that you know what I thought I knew.
It's the beat that my heart skips when I'm with you.
But I still don't understand just how your love
Can do what no one else can.

Refrain

Lookin' so crazy, your love's got me lookin',
Got me lookin' so crazy in love.

Rap:
Young Hov, y'all know when the flow is loco.
Young B and the R-O-C, uh-oh.
Ol' G, big homey, the one and only.
Stick bony, but the pocket is fat like Tony Soprano.
The ROC handles like Van Axel.
I shake phonies, man you can't
Get next to the genuine article, I do not sing low.

I sling though, if anything I bling yo'.
A star like Ringo, roar like a gringo.
Bret if you're crazy, bring your whole set.
Jay-Z in the range, crazy and deranged.
They can't figure him out, they like "Hey, is he insane?"
Yes sir, I'm cut from a different cloth.
My texture is the best fur chinchilla.
I been healin' the chain smokers.

How you think I got the name Hova?
I been realer, the game's over.
Fall back young, ever since the label changed
Over to platinum the game's been a wrap, one.

Sung:
Got me lookin' so crazy, my baby.
I'm not myself lately. I'm foolish, I don't do this.
I've been playin' myself. Baby, I don't' care.
'Cause your loves's got the best of me.
And baby you're makin' a fool of me.
You got me sprung and I don't care who sees.
'Cause baby you got me, you got me,
You got me so crazy right now.

Refrain

Don't Know Why

Words and Music by Jesse Harris

recorded by Norah Jones

I waited till I saw the sun.
I don't know why I didn't come.
I left you by the house of fun.
I don't know why I didn't come,
I don't know why I didn't come.

When I saw the break of day,
I wished that I could fly away
'Stead of kneeling in the sand
Catching teardrops in my hand.
My heart is drenched in wine.
But you'll be on my mind forever.

Out across the endless sea,
I would die in ecstasy.
But I'll be a bag of bones
Driving down the road alone.
My heart is drenched in wine,
But you'll be on my mind forever.

Something has to make you run.
I don't know why I didn't come.
I feel as empty as a drum.
I don't know why I didn't come,
I don't know why I didn't come.
I don't know why I didn't come.

Cry

Words and Music by Angie Aparo

recorded by Faith Hill

If I had just one tear runnin' down your cheek,
Maybe I could cope. Maybe I'd get some sleep.
If I had just one moment at your expense,
Maybe all my misery would be well spent, yeah.

Could you cry a little and lie just a little?
Pretend that you're feelin' a little more pain?
I gave, now I'm wantin' somethin' in return.
So, cry just a little for me.

If your love could be caged, honey,
I would hold the key and conceal it underneath
The pile of lies you handed me.
And you'd hunt and those lies,
They'd be all you'd ever find.
That'd be all you'd have to know
For me to be fine, yeah.

Can you cry a little and die just a little?
And baby, I would feel just a little less pain.
I gave, now I'm wantin' somethin' in return.
So, cry just a little for me.

Give it up, baby, I hear you're doin' fine.
Nothin's gonna save me and I see it in your eyes.
Some kind of heartache comin', give it a try.
I don't want pity, I just want what is mine, yeah.

Could you cry a little and lie just a little?
Pretend that you're feelin' a little more pain?
I gave, now I'm wantin' somethin' in return.
So, cry just a little for me, yeah.
Cry just a little for me.
Whoa, whoa, could you cry a little for me?

Dance with My Father

Words by Luther Vandross and Richard Marx
Music by Luther Vandross

recorded by Luther Vandross

Back when I was a child,
Before life removed all the innocence,
My father would lift me high
And dance with my mother and me
And then spin me around till I fell asleep,
Then up the stairs he would carry me.
And I knew for sure I was loved.

If I could get another chance,
Another walk, another dance with him,
I'd play a song that would never, ever end.
How I'd love, love, love
To dance with my father again.

When I and my mother would disagree,
To get my way I would run from her to him.
He'd make me laugh just to comfort me, yeah, yeah,
Then finally make me do just what my mama said.
Later that night when I was asleep,
He left a dollar under my sheet.
Never dreamed that he would be gone from me.

If I could steal one final glance,
One final step, one final dance with him,
I'd play a song that would never, ever end.
'Cause I'd love, love, love
To dance with my father again.

Sometimes I'd listen outside her door
And I'd hear how my mother cried for him.
I pray for her even more than me.
I pray for her even more than me.

I know I'm praying for much too much,
But could you send back the only man she loved?
I know you don't do it usually but, dear Lord,
She's dying to dance with my father again.
Every night I fall asleep and this is all I ever dream.

Disease

Words and Music by Rob Thomas and Mick Jagger

recorded by Matchbox Twenty

Feels like you made a mistake,
You made somebody's heart break.
But now I have to let you go.
I have to let you go.

You left a stain
On every one of my good days.
But I am stronger than you know.
I have to let you go.

No one's ever turned you over.
No one's tried to ever let you down.
Beautiful girl, bless your heart.
I've got a disease deep inside me,
Makes me feel uneasy baby.
I can't live without you.
Tell me what am I supposed to do about it?
Keep your distance from me.
Don't pay no attention to me.
I've got a disease.

Feels like you're makin' a mess.
You're hell on wheels in a black dress.
You drove me to the fire
And left me there to burn.

Every little thing you do is tragic.
All my life, the whole world's magic.
Beautiful girl, I can't breathe.
I got a disease deep inside me,
Makes me feel uneasy baby.
I can't live without you.
Tell me what am I supposed to do about it?
Keep your distance from me.
Don't pay no attention to me.
I got a disease.

And well I think that I'm sick, believe me.
Meanwhile, my world is comin' down on me.
You taste like honey, honey.
Tell me, can I be your honey?
Be, be strong, keep tellin' myself
That it won't take long till
I'm free of my disease.
Yeah, well, free of my disease.
Free of my disease, oh.

Yeah, well I got a disease deep inside me,
Makes me feel uneasy baby.
I can't live without you.
Tell me what am I supposed to do about it?
Keep your distance from me.
Don't pay no attention to me.
I got a disease.

And well I think that I'm sick, believe me.
Meanwhile, my world is comin' down on me.
You taste like honey, honey.
Tell me, can I be your honey?
Be, be strong, keep tellin' myself
That it won't take long till
I'm free of my disease.

Hey, I'm free of my disease.
Set me free of my disease.

Drift Away

Words and Music by Mentor Williams

recorded by Uncle Kracker featuring Dobie Gray

Day after day I'm more confused;
I look for the light in the pouring rain.
You know that's a game that I hate to lose.
I'm feelin' the strain; ain't it a shame?

Refrain:
Oh, give me the beat, boys, to soothe my soul;
I wanna get lost in your rock and roll and drift away.
Give me the beat, boys, to soothe my soul;
I wanna get lost in your rock and roll and drift away.

Beginning to think that I'm wastin' time;
Don't understand the things that I do.
'Cause the world outside looks so unkind.
Now I'm countin' on you to carry me through.

Refrain

And when my mind is free
No melody can move me.
When I'm feelin' blue
Guitars are comin' through to soothe me.

And thanks for the joy that you've given me;
I want you to know I believe in your song,
And rhythm and rhyme and harmony.
You help me along, makin' me strong.

Refrain

Fall to Pieces

Words and Music by Scott Weiland, Slash, Duff McKagan,
  Matt Sorum and Dave Kushner

recorded by Velvet Revolver

It's been a long year since you've been gone.
I've been alone here, I've grown old.
Fall to pieces, I'm fallin'.
Fell to pieces, and I'm still fallin'.
Every time, I'm fallin' down.
All alone I fall to pieces.

I keep a journal of memories.
I'm feelin' lonely, I can't breathe.
Fall to pieces, I'm fallin'.
Fell to pieces and I'm still fallin'.
Every time, I'm fallin' down.
All alone I fall to pieces.

Refrain:
Every time, I'm fallin' down.
All alone I fall to pieces.
Every time, I'm fallin' down.
All alone I fall to pieces.

All the years I've tried with more to go.
And will the mem'ries die?
I'm waiting. And will I find you?
And can I find you?
We're falling down, I'm falling.

Refrain Twice

Drive

Words and Music by Brandon Boyd, Michael Einziger, Alex Katunich,
Jose Pasillas II and Chris Kilmore

recorded by Incubus

Sometimes, I feel the fear
Of the uncertainty stinging clear.
And I can't help but ask myself
How much I'll let the fear take the wheel and steer.

It's driven me before
And it seems to have a vague haunting mass appeal.
But lately I'm beginning to find
That I should be the one behind the wheel.

Refrain:
Whatever tomorrow brings I'll be there
With open arms and open eyes, yeah!
Whatever tomorrow brings I'll be there,
I'll be there.

So if I decide to waiver my chance
To be one of the hive.
Will I choose water over wine
And hold my own and drive, ah, ah, ah, ah, oh?

It's driven me before and it seems to be the way
That everyone else gets around.
Lately I'm beginning to find that when
I drive myself my light is found.

Refrain

Would you choose water over wine,
Hold the wheel and drive?

Refrain

Do, do, do, do, do, do, do, do, do, do, do,
Bom, bom, bom, do, do, do, do, do.
Do, do, do, do, do, do, do, do, do, do, do,
Bom, bom, bom, bom, bom.

Drops of Jupiter (Tell Me)

Words and Music by Pat Monahan, Jimmy Stafford, Rob Hotchkiss,
Charlie Colin and Scott Underwood

recorded by Train

Now that she's back in the atmosphere
With drops of Jupiter in her hair, hey, hey,
She acts like summer and walks like rain,
Reminds me that there's a time to change, hey, hey.
Since the return from her stay on the moon,
She listens like spring and she talks like June.
Hey, hey, hey, hey.

But tell me, did you sail across the sun?
Did you make it to the Milky Way
To see that lights all faded
And that heaven is overrated?
Tell me, did you fall for a shooting star,
One without a permanent scar?
And did you miss me
While you were looking for yourself out there?

Now that she's back from that soul vacation,
Tracing her way through the constellation, hey, hey.
She checks out Mozart while she does Tae Bo,
Reminds me that there's room to grow, hey, hey.
Now that she's back in the atmosphere
I'm afraid that she might think of me
As plain old Jane, told a story 'bout a man
Who was too afraid to fly so he never did land.

But tell me, did the wind sweep you off your feet?
Did you finally get the chance to dance
Along the light of day,
And head back to the Milky Way?
And tell me, did Venus blow your mind?
Was it everything you wanted to find
And did you miss me
While you were looking for yourself out there?

Can you imagine no love, pride, deep fried chicken?
Your best friend always sticking up for you,
Even when I know you're wrong?
Can you imagine no first dance? Freeze dried? Romance?
Five hour phone conversation?

But tell me, did the wind sweep you off your feet?
Did you finally get the chance to dance
Along the light of day,
And head back toward the Milky Way?

But tell me, did you sail across the sun?
Did you make it to the Milky Way
To see that lights all faded
And that heaven is overrated?
Tell me, did you fall for a shooting star,
One without a permanent scar?
And did you miss me
While you were looking for yourself?

Na, na, na, na, na, na, na, na, na, na, na, na,
Na, na, na, na.
And did you finally get the chance to dance
Along the light of day?
Na, na, na, na, na, na, na, na, na, na, na, na,
Na, na, na, na.
And did you fall from a shooting star,
Fall from a shooting star?
Na, na, na, na, na, na, na, na, na, na, na, na,
Are you lonely looking for yourself out there?

Everything

Words and Music by Alanis Morissette

recorded by Alanis Morissette

I can be an asshole of the grandest kind.
I can withhold like it's going out of style.
I can be the moodiest baby.
And you've never met anyone who's
As negative as I am sometimes.

I am the wisest woman you've ever met.
I am the kindest soul with whom you've connected.
I have the bravest heart that you've ever seen
And you've never met anyone who's as positive
As I am sometimes.

Refrain:
You see everything. You see every part.
You see all my light and you love all my dark.
You dig everything of which I'm ashamed.
There's not anything to which you can't relate
And you're still here.

I blame everyone else, not my own partaking.
My passive aggressiveness can be devastating.
I'm the most gorgeous woman that you've ever known
And you've never met anyone who's as everything
As I am sometimes.

Refrain

What I resist, persists and speaks louder than I know.
But I resist your love no matter how low or high I go.

Refrain

You see everything. You see every part.
And you're still here.
You see all my light and you love my dark.
You dig every thing of which I'm ashamed.
There's not anything to which you can't relate.
And you're still here.

Everywhere

Words and Music by John Shanks and Michelle Branch

recorded by Michelle Branch

Turn it inside out so I can see
The part of you that's driftin' over me.
And when I wake you're, you're never there.
And when I sleep you're you're everywhere.
You're everywhere.

Just tell me how I got this far.
Just tell me why you're here and who you are.
'Cause every time I look you're always there.
And every time I sleep you're always there.

Refrain:
'Cause you're everywhere to me.
And when I close my eyes it's you I see.
You're everything I know.
That makes me believe I'm not alone.
I'm not alone.

I recognize the way you make me feel.
It's hard to think that you might not be real.
I sense it now, the water's getting deep.
I try to wash the pain away from me, away from me.

Refrain

When I touch your hand, it's then I understand
The beauty that's within. It's now that we begin.
You always light my way. I hope there never comes a day.
No matter where I go I always feel you so.

'Cause you're everywhere to me.
And when I close my eyes it's you I see.
You're everything I know.
That makes me believe I'm not alone.

'Cause you're everywhere to me.
And when I catch my breath it's you I breathe.
You're everything I know.
That makes me believe I'm not alone.
I'm not alone.
Oh, you're everyone I see. So tell me, do you see me?

Fallen

Words and Music by Sarah McLachlan

recorded by Sarah McLachlan

Heaven, bend to take my hand
And lead me through the fire.
Be the long awaited answer
To a long and painful fight.
Truth be told, I've tried my best,
But somewhere along the way
I got caught up in all there was to offer,
And the cost was so much more than I could bear.

Though I've tried, I've fallen.
I have sunk so low. I've messed up.
Better I should know, so don't come 'round here
And tell me I told you so.

We all begin with good intent.
Love was raw and young.
We believed that we could change ourselves,
The past can be undone.
But we carry on our back
The burden time always reveals
In the lonely light of morning,
In the wound that would not heal.
It's the bitter taste of losing ev'rything
That I've held so dear.

I've fallen.
I have sunk so low. I've messed up.
Better I should know, so don't come 'round here
And tell me I told you so, no.

Heaven, bend to take my hand,
I've nowhere left to turn.
I'm lost to those I thought were friends,
To everyone I know.
Oh, they turn their head, embarrassed,
Pretend that they don't see,
But it's one misstep, one slip before you know it,
And there doesn't seem a way to be redeemed.

Though I've tired, I've fallen.
I have sunk so low. I've messed up.
Better I should know, so don't come 'round here
And tell me I told you so.
And oh, I've messed up.
Better I should know, so don't come 'round here
And tell me I told you so.

Fallin'

Words and Music by Alicia Keys

recorded by Alicia Keys

I keep on fallin' in and out of love with-a you.
Sometimes I love you, sometimes you make me blue.
Sometimes I feel good. At times I feel used.
Loving you darling makes me so confused.
I keep on fallin' in and out of love with-a you.

I never loved someone the way that I love a-you.
Oh, oh, I never felt this-a way.
How do you give me so much pleasure
And cause me so much pain? Yeah, yeah.
Just when I think I'm taking more than would a fool,
I start fallin' back in love with you.

I keep on fallin' in and out of love with-a you.
I never loved someone the way that I love-a you.
Oh baby. I, I, I, I'm fallin'. I, I, I, I'm fallin'.
Fall, fall, fall.

I keep on fallin' in and out of love with-a you.
I never loved someone the way that I love-a you.
I'm fallin' in and out of love with-a you.
I never loved someone the way that I love-a you.
I'm fallin' in and out of love with-a you.
I never loved someone the way that I love-a you.

Spoken: What?

Freedom

Words and Music by Paul McCartney

recorded by Paul McCartney

This is my right, a right given by God,
To live a free life, to live in freedom.
Talking about freedom, I'm talking about freedom,
I will fight for the right to live in freedom.

Anyone who tries to take it away,
Will have to answer, 'cause this is my life.
Talking about freedom, I'm talking about freedom,
I will fight for the right to live in freedom.

Talking about freedom, I'm talking about freedom,
I will fight for the right to live in freedom.
Everybody talking about freedom, I'm talking about freedom,
I will fight for the right to live in freedom.

Talking about freedom, I'm talking about freedom,
I will fight for the right to live in freedom.
Everybody talking about freedom, I'm talking about freedom,
I will fight for the right to live in freedom.

Fat Lip

Words and Music by Sum 41

recorded by Sum 41

Spoken:
Storming through the party like my name is El Niño,
When I'm hanging out drinking in the back of an El Camino.
As a kid was a skid and no one knew me by name.
Trashed my own house party 'cause nobody came.

Sung:
Well I know I'm not the one you thought you knew back in high
    school,
Never going, never showing up when we had to.
Attention that we crave, don't tell us to behave.
I'm sick of always hearing "act your age."

Refrain:
I don't wanna waste my time,
Become another casualty of society.
I'll never fall in line,
Become another victim of your conformity and back down.

Spoken:
Because you don't know us at all, we laugh when people fall.
But what would you expect with a conscience so small.
Heavy metal and mullets that's how we were raised.
Maiden and Priest were the gods that we praised.

Sung:
'Cause we like having fun at other people's expenses.
Cutting people down is just a minor offense then.
It's none of your concern. I guess I'll never learn.
I'm sick of being told to wait my turn.

Refrain

Don't count on me to let you know when.
Don't count on me, I'll do it again.
Don't count on me, it's the point you're missing.
Don't count on me, 'cause I'm not listening.

Spoken:
Well, I'm a no good-nick lower middle class brat.
Backpacked and I don't give a shit about nothing.
You be standing on the corner talking all that kufuffin,
But you don't make sense from all the gas you be huffing.
'Cause if the egg don't stain you'll be ringing off the hook.
You're on the hit list wanted in the telephone book.
I like songs with distortion. To drink in proportion.
The dentist said my mom should have had an abortion.
(…bortion…bortion…bortion…bortion)

Refrain

Waste my time with them.
Casualty of society.
Waste my time with them.
Victim of your conformity and back down.

Flavor of the Weak

Words and Music by Stacy Jones

recorded by American Hi-Fi

She paints her nails and she don't know
He's got her best friend on the phone.
She'll wash her hair, his dirty clothes
Are all he gives to her.
And he's got posters on the wall
Of all the girls he wished she was,
And he means everything to her.

Refrain:
Her boyfriend, he don't know anything about her.
He's too stoned, Nintendo.
I wish that I could make her see
She's just the flavor of the weak.

It's Friday night and she's all alone.
He's a million miles away.
She's dressed to kill but the TV's on.
He's connected to the sound.
And he's got pictures on the wall
Of all the girls he's loved before,
And she know all his favorite songs.

Refrain

Her boyfriend, he don't know anything about her.
He's too stoned. He's too stoned.
He's too stoned. He's too stoned.

Refrain

Yeah, she's the flavor of the weak,
And she makes me weak.

Float On

Words and Music by Isaac Brock, Eric Judy and Dann Gallucci

recorded by Modest Mouse

I backed my car into a cop car the other day.
Well, he just drove off, sometimes life's O.K.
I ran my mouth off a bit too much, oh, what did I say?
Well, you just laughed it off, it was all O.K.

And we'll all float on O.K.
And we'll all float on O.K.
And we'll all float on O.K.
And we'll all float on anyway.

Well, a fake Jamaican took every last dime with that scam.
It was worth it just to learn some sleight of hand.
Bad news comes, don't you worry even, and, when it land.
Good news will work its way to all them plans.

We both got fired on exactly the same day.
Well, we'll float on, good news is on the way.
Please come, please come good news, good news,
Good news, good news, good news coming.
Going to, how well? I can't tell.

And we'll all float on O.K.
And we'll all float on O.K.
And we'll all float on O.K.
And we'll all float on.

Alright already, we'll all float on.
No, don't you worry we'll all float on.
Alright already, we'll all float on.
Alright , don't worry we'll all float on.

Alright already. And we'll all float on.
Alright already, we'll all float on.
Alright, don't worry even if things end up a bit too heavy.
We'll all float on.

Alright already, we'll all float on.
Alright already we'll all float on O.K.
Don't worry, we'll all float on.
Even if things get heavy, we'll all float on.

Alright already, we'll all float on all…
All, alright. Don't you worry, we'll all float on.
We'll all float on.

Flying Without Wings

Words and Music by Wayne Hector and Steve Mac

recorded by Ruben Studdard

Everybody's looking for that something.
One thing that makes it all complete.
You'll find it in the strangest places.
Places you never knew it could be.

Some find it in the faces of their children.
Some find it in their lover's eyes.
Who can deny the joy it brings?
When you find that special thing
You're flying without wings.

Some find it sharing every morning,
Some in their solitary lives.
You'll find it in the words of others.
A simple line can make you laugh or cry.

You'll find it in the deepest friendships.
The kind you cherish all your life.
And when you know how much that means
You've found that special thing.
You're flying without wings.

So impossible as they may seem,
You've got to fight for every dream.
'Cause who's to know which one you let go
Would have made you complete?

But for me it's waking up beside you, yeah,
To watch the sunrise on your face.
To know that I can say I love you
At any given time or place, oh.

It's the little things that only I know.
Those are the things that make you mine, all mine.
And it's the flying without wings,
'Cause you're my special thing. I'm flying without wings.

You're the place my life begins
And you'll be where it ends.
I'm flying without wings and that's the joy it brings.
I'm flying without wings

Foolish

Words and Music by Irving Lorenzo and A. Douglas

recorded by Ashanti

Whispered: Murder Inc. Ashanti.

Refrain (Sung Twice):
See my days are cold without you
But I'm hurtin' while I'm with you.
And thought my heart can't take no more,
I keep on running back to you.

Baby, I don't know why you're treatin' me so bad.
You said you loved me, no one above me and I was all you had
And though my heart is beatin' for you I can't stop cryin'.
I don't know how I allow you to treat me this way and still I stay.

Refrain Twice

Baby, I don't know why you wanna do me wrong.
See when I'm home, I'm all alone and you are always gone.
And boy you know I really love you, I can't deny.
I can't see how you could bring me to so many tears
After all these years.

Refrain twice

Ooh, I trusted you. I trusted you.
So sad, so sad what love will make you do.
All the things that we accept be the things that we regret.
So all of my ladies, ladies tell me, come on, sing with me.

See, when I get the strength to leave
You always tell me that you need me.
And I'm weak 'cause I believe you.
And I'm mad because I love you.

So I stop and think that maybe
You could learn to 'preciate me.
Then it all remains the same
That you ain't never gonna change.
Never gonna change.

Refrain Twice

Baby, why you hurt me, leave me and desert me?
Boy I gave you all my heart and all you did was tear it up.
Lookin' out my window, knowin' that I should go.
Hate it when I pack my bags,
There's somethin' always holds me back.

Forever and for Always

Words and Music by Shania Twain and R.J. Lange

recorded by Shania Twain

Oh, I can hear your heart beat now.
I can hear it beating loud.
In your arms I can still feel
The way you want me when you hold me.
I can still hear the words you whispered when you told me
I can stay right here forever in your arms.

And there ain't no way I'm lettin' you go now.
And there ain't no way and there ain't no how.
Never see that day.
'Cause I'm keeping you forever and for always.
We will be together all of our days.
Wanna wake up every morning to your sweet face,
Always. Umm, baby.

In your heart I can still hear a beat
For every time you kiss me.
And when we're apart
I know how much you miss me.
I can feel your love for me in your heart.

And there ain't no way I'm lettin' you go now.
And there ain't no way and there ain't no how.
Never see that day.
'Cause I'm keeping you forever and for always.
We will be together all of our days.
Wanna wake up every morning to your sweet face,
Always. Ahh, wanna wake up every morning with you.

In your eyes I can still see
The look of the one who really loves me.
The one who wouldn't put anything else
In the world above me.
I can still see your love for me in your eyes.

And there ain't no way I'm lettin' you go now.
And there ain't no way and there ain't no how.
Never see that day.
'Cause I'm keeping you forever and for always.
We will be together all of our days.
Wanna wake up every morning to your sweet face.
I'm keeping you forever and for always.

We will be together all of our days.
Wanna wake up every morning to your sweet face.
I'm keeping you forever and for always.
Ahh, I'm keeping you forever.
But you keep me waiting, ahh, umm,
Here forever in your arms.

The Game of Love

Words and Music by Rick Nowels and Gregg Alexander

recorded by Santana featuring Michelle Branch

Tell me just what you want me to be.
One kiss and boom, you're the only one for me.
So please tell me why don't you come around no more?
'Cause right now I'm crying outside the door
Of your candy store.

Refrain:
It just takes a little bit of this. A little bit of that.
It started with a kiss, now we're up to bat.
A little bit of laughs. A little bit of pain.
I'm telling you, my babe, it's all in the game of love.

Love is whatever you make it to be.
Sunshine set on his cold lonely sea.
So please baby try and use me for what I'm good for.
It ain't sayin' goodbye that's knockin' down the door
Of your candy store.

Refrain

It's all in this game of love.
You roll me, control me, console me.
Please hold me.
You guide me, divide me into what…
(Make me feel good, yeah.)

So please tell me why don't you come around no more?
'Cause right now I'm dying outside the door
Of your loving store.

Refrain

Repeat and Fade:
A little bit of this. A little bit of that.
A little bit of laughs. A little bit of pain.

Get the Party Started

Words and Music by Linda Perry

recorded by Pink

I'm comin' up so you better get this party started.
I'm comin' up so you better get this party started.

Get this party started on a Saturday night.
Everybody's waitin' for me to arrive.
Sendin' out the message to all of my friends.
We'll be lookin' flashy in my Mercedes Benz.
I get lots of style, got my diamond rings.
I can go for miles if you know what I mean.

I'm comin' up so better get this party started.
I'm coming up, I'm comin'.
I'm comin' up so you better get this party started.

Pumpin' up the volume, breakin' down to the beat.
Cruisin' through the west side we'll be checkin' the scene.
Boulevard is freakin' as I'm comin' up fast.
I'll be burnin' rubber, you'll be kissin' my ass.
Pull up to the bumper, get out of the car.
License plate says "Stunner Number One Superstar."

I'm comin' up so better get this party started.
I'm coming up, I'm comin'.
I'm comin' up so you better get this party started.
Get this party started.

Makin' my connection as I enter the room.
Everybody's chillin' as I set up the groove.
Pumpin' up the volume with this brand new beat.
Everybody's dancin' and they're dancin' for me.
I'm your operator, you can call anytime.
I'll be your connection to the party line.

I'm comin' up so better get this party started.
I'm comin' up, uh huh.
I'm comin' up so better get this party started.
I'm comin' up, I'm comin'.
I'm comin' up so better get this party started.
I'm comin' up, you better.
I'm comin' up so better get this party started.
Get this party started.

Girlfriend

Words and Music by Pharrell Williams, Chad Hugo and Justin Timberlake

recorded by 'N Sync

Spoken:
Would you like to be my girlfriend?
Would you be my girlfriend?
I like you right? Would you be my girlfriend?

Sung:
I don't know why you care.
He doesn't even know you're there, oh no.
'Cause he don't love your eyes
And he don't love your smile.
Girl, you know that ain't fair.

The middle of the night, is he gonna be by your side?
Or will he run and hide?
You don't know 'cause things ain't clear.
And baby when you cry is he gonna stand by your side?
Does the man even know you're alive?

I got an idea. Why don't you be my girlfriend?
I'll treat you good.
I know you hear your friends when they say you should.
'Cause if you were my girlfriend, I'd be your shining star.
The one to show you where you are.
Girl, you should be my girlfriend.

Does he know what you feel?
Are you sure that it's real, yeah?
Does he ease your mind?
Or does he break your stride?
Did you know that love could be a shield, yeah.

The middle of the night, is he gonna be by your side?
Or will he run and hide?
You don't know 'cause things ain't clear.
And baby when you cry is he gonna stand by your side?
Does the man even know you're alive?

I got an idea. Why don't you be my girlfriend?
I'll treat you good.
I know you hear your friends when they say you should.
'Cause if you were my girlfriend, I'd be your shining star.
The one to show you where you are.
Girl, you should be my girlfriend.

Ahh, ha, ha.

Ever since I saw your face
Nothing in my life has been the same.
I walk around just saying your name.
Without you my world would end, yeah.
I've searched around this whole damn place
And everything says you were meant to be my girlfriend, oh.

Why don't you be my girlfriend?
I'll treat you good.
I know you hear your friends when they say you should.
'Cause if you were my girlfriend, I'd be your shining star.
The one to show you where you are.
Girl, you should be my girlfriend.

Ahh, ha, ha. Ahh, ha,
Girl, you should be my girlfriend.
Girl, you should be my girlfriend.
Girl, you should be my girlfriend.
Girl, you should be my girlfriend.
Girl, you should be my girlfriend.
My girlfriend.

Heaven

Words and Music by Henry Garza, Joey Garza and Ringo Garza

recorded by Los Lonely Boys

Save me from this prison. Lord, help me get away.
'Cause only you can save me now from this misery.
I've been lost in my own place and I'm gettin' weary.
How far is heaven?
And I know that I need to change my ways of livin'.
How far is heaven? Lord, can you tell me?

I've been locked up way too long in this crazy world.
How far is heaven?
And I just keep on prayin', Lord, and just keep on livin'.
How far is heaven? Yeah, Lord, can you tell me?
How far is heaven? 'Cause I just gotta know how far, yeah.
How far is heaven? Yeah, Lord, can you tell me?

Tu que estas entrado al ciela.
Hecha me tu ben dicion.

'Cause I know there's a better place than this place I'm livin'.
How far is heaven?
And I just got to have some faith and just keep on givin'.
How far is heaven? Yeah, Lord, can you tell me?
How far is heaven? 'Cause I just gotta know how far, yeah.
How far is heaven? Yeah, Lord, can you tell me?

How far is heaven? 'Cause I just gotta know how far.
I just wanna know how far.

Give Me Just One Night (Una Noche)

Words and Music by Deetah, Anders Bagge and Arnthor Birgisson

recorded by 98 Degrees

Lips keep telling me you want me
And hold me close all through the night.
And I know that deep inside you need me.
No one else can make it right.

Don't you try to hide your secrets.
I can see it in your eyes.
You said the words without speaking.
Now I'm gonna make you mine.

Refrain:
Give me just one night, una noche.
A moment to be by your side.
Give me just one night, una noche.
I'll give you the time of your life,
The time of your life.
I'll give you the time of your life.

Your lust for passion makes me crazy.
Your existence makes me wild.
I wanna loosen up your feelings,
See what's hiding inside.

Refrain

Aye que rico me pone loca,
Como te mueves, como me toca.
Tu movimiento, tu sentimeinto,
Si yo te quiero te do la noche,
Today la noche, aye!

Give me just one night. Give me one night, baby.
A moment to be by your side.
Give me just one night.
Oh, just for one night, oh baby.
I'll give you the time of your life.
Give me just one night.

Refrain

Have a Nice Day

Words and Music by Jon Bon Jovi, Richie Sambora and John Shanks

recorded by Bon Jovi

Why you wanna tell me how to live my life?
Who are you to tell me if it's black or white?
Mama, can you help me try and understand,
Is innocence the difference 'tween a boy and a man?
My daddy lived a lie. That's just the price that he paid.
Sacrificed his life just slavin' away.

Refrain:
Ooh, if there's one thing I hang onto
That gets me through the night.
I ain't gonna do what I don't want to.
I'm gonna live my life.
Shinin' like a diamond, rollin' with the dice.
Standin' on the ledge I show the wind how to fly.
When the world gets in my face I say,
Have a nice day. Have a nice day.

Take a look around you, nothin's what it seems.
We're livin' in the broken home of hopes and dreams.
Let me be the first to shake a helpin' hand
Of anybody brave enough to take a stand.
I've knocked on every door down every dead end street
Lookin' for forgiveness in what's left to believe.

Refrain Twice

Have a nice day.
When the world keeps tryin' to drag me down,
Gotta raise my hand. Gonna stay my ground.
I say, hey, have a nice day.
Have a nice day. Have a nice day.

Here Without You

Words and Music by Matt Roberts, Brad Arnold, Christopher Henderson
and Robert Harrell

recorded by 3 Doors Down

A hundred days have made me older
Since the last time that I saw your pretty face.
A thousand lies have made me colder
And I don't think I can look at this the same.
But all the miles that separate,
They disappear now when I'm dreamin' of your face.

I'm here without you baby,
But you're still on my lonely mind.
I think about you, baby,
And I dream about you all the time.
I'm here without you, baby,
But you're still with me in my dreams.
And tonight it's only you and me, ohh.

The miles just keep rollin'
As the people leave their way to say hello.
I've heard this life is overrated
But I hope that it gets better as we go, oh yeah, yeah.

I'm here without you baby,
But you're still on my lonely mind.
I think about you, baby,
And I dream about you all the time.
I'm here without you, baby,
But you're still with me in my dreams.
And tonight girl, it's only you and me.

Everything I know and anywhere I go,
It gets hard but it won't take away my love.
And when the last one falls, when it's all said and done,
It gets hard but it won't take away my love, whoa.

I'm here without you baby,
But you're still on my lonely mind.
I think about you, baby,
And I dream about you all the time.
I'm here without you, baby,
But you're still with me in my dreams.
And tonight girl, it's only you and me.
Yeah, oh yeah, ohh, ohh.

Here's to the Night

Written by Max Collins, Jon Siebels and Tony Fagenson

recorded by Eve 6

So denied, so I lied.
Are you the now or never kind?
In a day and a day love
I'm gonna be gone for good again.
Are you willing to be had?
Are you cool with just tonight?

Refrain:
Here's a toast to all those who hear me all too well.
Here's to the night we felt alive.
Here's to the tears you knew you'd cry.
Here's to goodbye, tomorrow's gonna come too soon.

Put your name on the line
Along with place and time.
Wanna stay, not to go.
I wanna ditch the logical.

Refrain

All my time is froze in motion.
Can't I stay an hour or two more?
Don't let me let you go.
Don't let me let you go.

Refrain Twice

Independent Women Part I

Words and Music by Cory Rooney, Samuel Barnes,
  Jean Claude Olivier and Beyonce Knowles

from *Charlie's Angels*
recorded by Destiny's Child

Spoken:
Lucy Liu with my girl Drew
Cameron D. and Destiny,
Charlie's Angels come on.

Sung:
Question: Tell me what you think about me.
I buy my own diamonds and I buy my own rings.
Only ring your celly when I'm feelin' lonely.
When it's all over please get up and leave.

Question: Tell me how you feel about this.
Try to control me, boy, you get dismissed.
Pay my own car note and I pay my own bills.
Always fifty-fifty in relationships.

Refrain:
The shoes on my feet, I bought it.
The clothes I'm wearin', I bought it.
The rock I'm rockin', I bought it
'Cause I depend on me if I want it.
The watch I'm wearin', I bought it.
The house I live in, I bought it.
The car I'm drivin', I bought it.
I depend on me. I depend on me.

All the women who independent
Throw your hands up at me.
All the honeys who makin' money
Throw your hand up at me.
All the mommas who profit dollars
Throw your hands up at me.
All the ladies who truly feel me
Throw your hands up at me.
Girl, I didn't know you could get down like that.
Charlie, know your angels get down like that.
Girl, I didn't know you could get down like that.
Charlie, how your angels get down like that.

Tell me how you feel about this:
Who would I want if I would wanna live?
I worked hard and sacrificed to get what I get.
Ladies it ain't easy bein' independent.

Question: How'd you like this knowledge that I brought?
Braggin' on the cash that he gave us is the front.
If you're gonna brag make sure it's your money you flaunt.
Depend on no one else to give you what you want.

Refrain

Spoken:
Destiny's Child (Wass up!) you in the house?
(Sure nuff!) We'll break these people off angel style.

Sung:
Child of destiny, independent beauty.
No one else can scare me. Charlie's Angels.

All the women who independent throw your hands up at me.
All the honeys who makin' money throw your hand up at me.
All the mommas who profit dollars throw your hands up at me.
All the ladies who truly feel me throw your hands up at me.

Girl, I didn't know you could get down like that.
Charlie, how your angels get down like that.

Repeat and Fade:
Girl, I didn't know you could get down like that
Charlie, how your angels get down like that.

Hero

Words and Music by Enrique Iglesias, Paul Barry and Mark Taylor

recorded by Enrique Iglesias

There's a hero
If you look inside your heart.
You don't have to be afraid
Of what you are.
There's an answer
If you reach into your soul
And the sorrow that you know
Will melt away.

Refrain:
And then a hero comes along
With the strength to carry on
And you cast your fears aside
And you know you can survive.
So, when you feel like hope is gone
Look inside you and be strong
And you'll finally see the truth
That a hero lies in you.

It's a long road
When you face the world alone.
No one reaches out a hand
For you to hold.
You can find love
If you search within yourself
And the emptiness you felt
Will disappear.

Refrain

Lord knows
Dreams are hard to follow,
Don't let anyone tear them away.
Hold on,
There will be tomorrow.
In time you'll find the way.

Refrain

Hey Ya!

Words and Music by Andre Benjamin

recorded by Outkast

My baby don't mess around because she loves me so
And this I know for sure, uhh.
But does she really want to
But can't stand to see me walk out the door, uuh?
Don't try to fight the feelin'
'Cause the thought alone is killin me right now, uhh.
Thank God for Mom and Dad for sticking
Two together 'cause we don't know how, uhh.

Hey ya! Hey ya! Hey ya! Hey ya!
Hey ya! Hey ya! Hey ya! Hey ya!

You think you've got it. Oh, you think you've got it.
But got it just don't get it till there's nothing at all.
We get together. Oh, we get together.
But separate always when there's feelings involved.

If what they say is "nothing is forever,"
Then what makes, then what make, then what makes,
Then what makes, then what makes, huh, love the exception?
So why, oh? Why oh? Why oh? Why oh?
Why oh are we so in denial when we know we're not happy here?

Hey ya! Hey ya!
Don't want to meet your daddy, oh oh.
Just want you in my Caddy, oh, oh.
Oh, oh, don't want to meet your mama, oh, oh.
Just meant to make you cumma, oh, oh.
I'm, I'm, oh, oh, I'm just being honest.
Oh, oh, I'm just being honest.

Rap:

3000: Hey, alright now. Alright now fella!

Fellas: Yeah!

3000: Now, what's cooler than being cool?

Fellas: Ice Cold!

3000: I can't hear ya. I say what's, what's cooler than being cool?

Fellas: Ice Cold!

3000: Alright, alright, alright, alright,

Alright, alright, alright, alright.

Ok, now ladies.

Ladies: Yeah!

3000: Now, we gon' break this thing down in just a few second.

Now, don't have me break this thing down for nothin'.

Now, I wanna see y'all on y'all baddest behavior.

Lend me some sugar, I am your neighbor, ahh.

Here we go, uhh.

Sung:

Shake it. Shake, shake it. Shake it. Shake, shake it.

Shake it. Shake, shake it. Shake it. Shake it. Shake, shake it.

Shake it like a Polaroid picture.

Shake it Shake it. Shake, shake it.

Shake it. Shake, shake it. Shake it. Shake it. Shake, it sugar.

Shake it like a Polaroid picture. Shake it. Shake it.

Shake, shake it. Shake it. Shake , shake it. Shake it.

Shake it. Shake, shake it. Shake it like a Polaroid picture.

Rap:

Now all Beyonces and Lucy Lius

And Baby Dolls get on the floor.

You know what to do. You know what to do.

You know what to do.

Sung, repeat and fade:

Hey ya! Hey ya! Hey ya! Hey ya!

Home

Words and Music by Amy Foster-Gillies, Michael Bublé and Alan Chang

recorded by Michael Bublé

Another summer day has come and gone away
In Paris and Rome, but I wanna go home.
Maybe surrounded by a million people;
I still feel all alone, just wanna go home.
Oh, I miss you, you know.

I've been keeping all the letters that I wrote to you,
Each one a line or two, "I'm fine, baby, how are you?"
I would send them, but I know that it's just not enough.
My words were cold and flat, and you deserve more that that.

Another aeroplane, another sunny place;
I'm lucky, I know, but I wanna go home,
I've got to go home. Let me go home.
I'm just too far from where you are; I wanna come home.

And I feel just like I'm living someone else's life.
It's like I just stepped outside when everything was going right.
And I know just why you could not come along with me:
This was not your dream, but you always believed in me.

Another winter day has come and gone away
In either Paris or Rome, and I wanna go home, let me go home.
And I'm surrounded by a million people;
I, I still feel alone, and let me go home.

Oh, I miss you, you know. Let me go home.
I've had my run, and, baby, I'm done.
I've gotta go home. Let me go home.
It'll all be all right; I'll be home tonight.
I'm coming back home.

I Believe

Words and Music by Samuel Watters, Louis Biancaniello and Tamyra Gray

recorded by Fantasia

Have you ever reached a rainbow's end?
And did you find your pot of gold, umm?
Ever catch a shooting star?
And tell me how high did you soar?

Ever felt like you were dreaming
Just to find that you're awake?
And the magic that surrounds you
Can lift you up and guide you on your way.

I can see it in the stars across the sky.
Dreamt a hundred thousand dreams before,
Now I finally realize.
You see I've waited all my life for this moment to arrive
And finally I believe.

When you look out in the distance
You see it never was that far, oh, no.
Heaven knows you existence
And wants you to be ev'rything you are.

Ooh, there's a time for every soul to fly.
It's in the eyes of every child.
It's the hope that love can save the world.
And ooh, we should never let it go.

I can see it in the stars across the sky.
Dreamt a hundred thousand dreams before,
Now I finally realize.
You see I've waited all my life for this moment to arrive
And finally yeah, yeah, yeah, yeah, yeah, yeah.

I believe in the impossible
If I reach deep within my heart, yeah.
Overcome any obstacle, won't let this dream just fall apart.
You see I strive to be the very best.
Shine my light for all to see.
'Cause anything is possible when you believe.

I can see it in the stars across the sky.
Dreamt a hundred thousand dreams before,
Now I finally realize.
You see I've waited all my life for this moment to arrive
And finally I believe, oh, yeah. I believe, oh yeah.
Love keeps lifting me higher.
Love keeps lifting me higher.

Repeat and Fade:
Love keeps lifting me higher.

I Hope You Dance

Words and Music by Tia Sillers and Mark D. Sanders

recorded by Lee Ann Womack with Sons of the Desert

I hope you never lose your sense of wonder,
You get your fill to eat, but always keep that hunger.
May you never take one single breath for granted.
God forbid love ever leave you empty handed.
I hope you still feel small when you stand beside the ocean.
Whenever one door closes, I hope one more opens.
Promise me that you'll give faith a fighting chance.
And when you get the choice to sit it out or dance,
I hope you dance. I hope you dance.

I hope you never fear those mountains in the distance,
Never settle for the path of least resistance.
Livin' might mean takin' chances if they're worth takin'.
Lovin' might be a mistake, but it's worth makin'.
Don't let some hell-bent heart leave you bitter.
When you come close to sellin' out, reconsider.
Give the heavens above more than just a passing glance.
And when you get the choice to sit it out or dance,
I hope you dance. I hope you dance.

(Time is a wheel in constant motion, always rolling us along.
Tell me, who wants to look back on their youth
And wonder where those years have gone?)

I hope you still feel small when you stand beside the ocean.
Whenever one door closes, I hope one more opens.
Promise me that you'll give faith a fighting chance.
And when you get the choice to sit it out or dance,
Dance. I hope you dance.

(Time is a wheel in constant motion, always rolling us along.
Tell me, who wants to look back on their youth
And wonder where those years have gone?)

I'm with You

Words and Music by Avril Lavigne, Lauren Christy, Scott Spock and Graham Edwards

recorded by Avril Lavigne

I'm standing on the bridge.
I'm waiting in the dark.
I thought that you'd be here by now,
There's nothing but the rain.
No footsteps on the ground.
I'm listening but there's no sound.

Refrain:
Isn't anyone tryin' to find me?
Won't somebody come take me home?
It's a damn cold night tryin' to figure out this life,
Won't you take me by the hand,
Take me somewhere new.
I don't know who you are but I, I'm with you.
I'm with you, umm.

I'm looking for a place
I'm searching for a face.
Is anybody here I know?
'Cause nothing's going right
And everything's a mess.
And no one likes to be alone.

Refrain

Oh, why is everything so confusing?
Maybe I'm just out of my mind,
Yeah, yeah, yeah, yeah, yeah, yeah.
It's a damn cold night tryin' to figure out this life.
Won't you take me by the hand,
Take me somewhere new.
I don't know who you are but I, I'm with you.
I'm with you.

Take me by the hand take me somewhere new.
I don't know who you are but I, I'm, with you.
I'm with you.

Take me by the hand take me somewhere new.
I don't know who you are but I, I'm with you,
Oh, I'm with you. I'm with you.

If You're Gone

Written by Rob Thomas

recorded by Matchbox Twenty

I think I've already lost you.
I think you're already gone.
I think I'm finally scared now.
You think I'm weak, I think you're wrong.

I think you're already leaving.
Feels like your hand is on the door.
I thought this place was an empire.
Now I'm relaxed. I can't be sure.

And I think you're so mean. I think we should try.
I think I could need this in my life and I think I'm scared.
I think too much. I know it's wrong. It's a problem I'm dealing.
If you're gone, maybe it's time to come home.

There's an awful lot of breathing room,
But I can hardly move.
If you're gone, baby, you need to come home, come home.
There's a little bit of something me in everything in you.

I bet you're hard to get over.
I bet the room just won't shine.
I bet my hands I can stay here
And I bet you need more than you mind.

And I think you're so mean. I think we should try.
I think I could need this in my life.
I think I'm just scared that I know too much.
I can't relate and that's a problem I'm feeling.
If you're gone, maybe it's time to come home.

There's an awful lot of breathing room,
But I can hardly move.
If you're gone, baby, you need to come home, come home.
There's a little bit of something me in everything in you.

I think you're so mean. I think we should try.
I think I could need this in my life and I think I'm scared.
Do I talk too much? I know it's wrong.
It's a problem I'm dealing.
If you're gone, then maybe it's time to come home.

Well, there's an awful lot of breathing room,
But I can hardly move.
You know, if you're gone, hell, baby,
You need to come home, ooh, come home.

There's a little bit of something me in everything in you.
Something in me, everything in.
Something in me in you.

Incomplete

Words and Music by Montell Jordan, Anthony Crawford and Kristin Hudson

recorded by Sisqo

Bright lights, fancy restaurants.
Everything in this world that a man could want.
Got a bank account bigger than the law should allow.
Still, I'm lonely now.
Pretty faces from the covers of the magazines.
From their covers to my covers wanna lay with me.
Fame and fortune, still I find,
Just a grown man runnin' out of time.

Refrain:
Even though it seems I have everything,
I don't wanna be a lonely fool.
All of the women, all the expensive cars,
All of the money don't amount to you.
So I can make believe I have ev'rything.
But I can't pretend that I don't see
That without you, girl, my life is incomplete.
Said without you, girl.

Your perfume, your sexy lingerie.
Girl, I remember it just like it was on yesterday,
A Thursday, you told me you had fallen in love.
I wasn't sure that I was.

S'been a year, winter, summer, spring, and fall.
But bein' without you just ain't livin' at all.
If I could travel back in time,
I'd relive the days you were mine.
Even though it out you girl I just can't help lovin' you.
But I loved you much too late.
I'd give anything and everything
To hear you say that you'll stay.

Refrain Twice

Without you girl my life is incomplete,
Yeah, my life is incomplete.

Inside Your Heaven

Words and Music by Savan Kotecha, Per Nylen and Andreas Carlsson

recorded by Carrie Underwood, Bo Bice

I've been down, now I'm blessed.
I felt a revelation comin' around.
Guess it's right, it's so amazing.
Every time I see you I'm alive.
You're all I've got. You lift me up.
The sun and the moonlight,
All my dreams are in your eyes.

Refrain:
And I wanna be inside your heaven.
Take me to the place you cry from
When a storm blows you away.
And I wanna be the earth that holds you.
Every bit of air you're breathing' in,
A soothin' wind.

I wanna be inside your heaven when we touch.
When we love the stars line up,
The wrong becomes undone.
Naturally my soul surrenders.
The sun and the moonlight,
All my dreams are in your eyes.

Refrain

I wanna be inside your heaven.
When minutes turn to days and years.
If mountains fall I'll still be here,
Holding you until the day I die.

And I wanna be inside your heaven.
Take me to the place you cry from
When a storm blows you away.
I wanna be inside your heaven.
Take me to the place you cry from
When a storm blows you away.

Refrain

I wanna be inside your heaven.

Intuition

Lyrics by Jewel Kilcher
Music by Jewel Kilcher and Lester A. Mendez

recorded by Jewel

La di da da. La di da da.
La di da da, la la.

I'm just a simple girl
In a high tech digital world.
Really try to understand
All the powers that rule this land.

They say Miss J.'s big butt is boss.
Kate Moss can't find a job.
In a world of post modern fad
What was good now is bad.
It's not hard to understand.
Just follow this simple plan:

Refrain:
Follow your heart, your intuition.
It will lead you in the right direction.
Let go of your mind.
Your intuition is easy to find.
Just follow your heart, baby.

La di da da. La di da da.
La di da da, la la.

You look at me but you're not quite sure.
Am I it or could you get more?
You learn cool from magazines.
You learned love from Charlie Sheen.
If you want me let me know
I promise I won't say no.

Refrain

You've got somethin' that you want me to sell.
Sell your sin. Just cash it in.
You've got somethin' that you want me to tell.
You'll love me, wait and see.
If you want me don't play games.
I promise it won't be in vain.

Refrain Four Times

Follow your heart, your intuition.
It will lead you in the right direction.

Jenny from the Block

Words and Music by Troy Oliver, Andre Deyo, Jennifer Lopez, Jean Claude Olivier,
    Samuel Barnes, Jose Fernando Arbex Miro, Lawrence Parker, Scott Sterling,
    M. Oliver, David Styles and Jason Phillips

recorded by Jennifer Lopez featuring Jadakiss and Styles

Children grow and women producing.
Men go working, some go stealing.
Ev'ryone's got to make a living.

Spoken:
L.O.X., yeah. J. Lo, yeah, yeah, yo, yo.

Rap:
We off the blocks this year.
Went from a 'lil to a lot this year.
Everybody mad at the rocks that I wear.
I know where I'm goin' and I know where I'm from.
You hear LOX in the air. Yeah we at the airport out.
D-block from the block where everybody air forced out.
Wit' a new white tee you fresh. Nothin' phony wit' us.
Make the money, get the mansion, bring the homies wit' us.

Refrain, sung:
Don't be fooled by the rocks that I got.
I'm still, I'm still Jenny from the block.
Used to have a little, now I have a lot.
No matter where I go I know where I came from.
Don't be fooled by the rocks that I got.
I'm still, I'm still Jenny from the block.

Used to have a little, now I have a lot.
No matter where I go I know where I came from,
From the Bronx.

From "In Living Color" to movie scripts
To "on the Six" to "J. Lo" this, headline clips.
I stay grounded as the amounts roll in.
I'm real, I thought I told ya.
I'm real even on Oprah. That's just me.
Nothin' phony, don't hate on me.
What you get is what you see.

Refrain

I'm down to earth like this. Rockin' this business.
I've grown up so much. I'm in control and lovin' it.
Rumors got me laughin', kid. I love my life and my public.
Put God first and can't forget to stay real.
To me it's like breathing, yeah.

Refrain

Rap:
Yo, it take hard work to cash checks
So don't be fooled by the rocks that I got, they're assests.
You get back what you put out.
Even if you take the good route, can't count the hood out.
After a while you'll know who to blend wit'.
Just keep it real wit' the ones you came in wit'.
Best thing to do is stay low, LOX and J. Lo.
They act like they don't but they know.
Sung: Everyone's got to make a living.

Refrain Four Times

Kryptonite

Words and Music by Matt Roberts, Brad Arnold and Todd Harrell

recorded by 3 Doors Down

Well, I took a walk around the world
To ease my troubled mind.
I left my body lying somewhere
In the sands of time.
But I watched the world float
To the dark side of the moon.
I feel there's nothing I can do. Yeah.

I watched the world float
To the dark side of the moon.
After all, I knew it had to be
Something to do with you.
I really don't mind what happens now and then,
As long as you'll be my friend at the end.

Refrain:
Well, if I go crazy,
Then will you still call me Superman?
If I'm alive and, well,
Will you be there holding my hand?
I'll keep you by my side
With my super human might.
Kryptonite.

You called me strong, you called me weak,
But still your secrets I will keep.
You took for granted all the times
I never let you down.
You stumbled in and bumped your head.
If not for me, then you'd be dead.
I picked you up and put you back on solid ground.

Refrain Twice

Learn to Fly

Words and Music by Dave Grohl, Nate Mendel and Taylor Hawkins

recorded by Foo Fighters

Run and tell all of the angels this could take all night.
Think I need a devil to help me get things right.
Hook me up a new revolution 'cause this one is a lie.
We sat around laughin' and watched the last one die.

I'm lookin' to the sky to save me, lookin' for a sign of life,
Lookin' for somethin' to help me burn out bright.
I'm lookin' for a complication, lookin' 'cause I'm tired of lyin'.
Make my way back home when I learn to fly high.

Think I'm dyin' nursin' patience. It can wait one night.
Give it all away if you give me one last try.
We'll live happily ever trapped if you just save my life.
Run and tell the angels that everything's all right.

I'm lookin' to the sky to save me, lookin' for a sign of life,
Lookin' for somethin' to help me burn out bright.
I'm lookin' for a complication, lookin' 'cause I'm tired of tryin'.
Make my way back home when I learn to fly high.
Make my way back home when I learn to…

Fly along with me. I can't quite make it alone.
Try to make this life my own.
Fly along with me. I can't quite make it alone.
Try to make this life my own.

I look into the sky to save me, lookin' for a sign of life,
Lookin' for somethin' to help me burn out bright.
I'm lookin' for a complication, lookin' 'cause I'm tired of tryin'.
Make my way back home when I learn to…

I look into the sky to save me, lookin' for a sign of life,
Lookin' for somethin' to help me burn out bright.
I'm lookin' for a complication, lookin' 'cause I'm tired of tryin'.
Make my way back home when I learn to fly high.

Make my way back home when I learn to fly.
Make my way back home when I learn to…

Lifestyles of the Rich and Famous

Words and Music by Benji Madden and Joel Madden

recorded by Good Charlotte

Always see it on T.V. or read it in the magazines,
Celebrities that want sympathy.
All they do is piss and moan inside the *Rolling Stone*,
Talking about how hard life can be.

I'd like to see them spend a week
Livin' life out on the street.
I don't think they would survive.
If they could spend a day or two
Walking in someone else's shoes
I think they'd stumble and they'd fall.
They would fall, fall.

Lifestyles of the rich and famous.
They're always complaining, always complaining.
If money is such a problem, well they got mansions
Think we should rob them.

Did you know when you were famous you could kill your wife?
And there's no such thing as twenty-five to life
As long as you got the cash to pay for Cochran.
And did you know if you were caught and you were smoking crack,
McDonald's wouldn't even want to take you back?
You could always just run for mayor of D.C.

I'd like to see them spend a week
Livin' life out on the street.
I don't think they would survive.
If they could spend a day or two
Walking in someone else's shoes
I think they'd stumble and they'd fall.
They would fall.

Lifestyles of the rich and famous.
They're always complaining, always complaining.
If money is such a problem, well they got mansions
Think we should rob them, rob them, rob them.
They would fall, fall.

Lifestyles of the rich and famous.
They're always complaining, always complaining.
If money is such a problem, you got so many problems,
Think I can solve them.

Lifestyles of the rich and famous.
We'll take the clothes, cash, cars and homes,
Just stop complaining.
Lifestyles of the rich and famous.
Lifestyles of the rich and famous.
Lifestyles of the rich and famous.

Lonely No More

Words and Music by Rob Thomas

recorded by Rob Thomas

Now it seems to me that you know just what to say.
But words are only words.
Can you show me something else?
Can you swear to me that you'll always be this way?
Show me how you feel more than ever,
Baby, baby, baby, baby.

Refrain:
Well, I don't wanna be lonely no more.
I don't wanna have to pay for this.
I don't want to know the lover at my door
Is just another heartache on my list.
I don't want to be angry no more.
And you know I could never stand for this.
So when you tell me that you love me, know for sure,
I don't want to be lonely anymore.
Ooh, ooh, ooh. Ooh, ooh, ooh.

Now it's hard for me when my heart's still on the mend.
Open up to me like you do you girlfriends.
And you sing to me and it's harmony.
Girl, what you do to me is everything.
Let me try anything just to get you back again.
Why can't we just try.

Refrain

What if I was good to you?
What if you were good to me?
What if I could hold you
'Til I feel you move inside of me?
And what if it was paradise?
And what if we were symphonies?
What if I gave all my life
To find some way to stand beside you?

Refrain

I don't wanna be lonely anymore.
Ooh, ooh, ooh, ooh. Ooh, ooh,
I don't wanna be lonely anymore.

Making Memories of Us

Words and Music by Rodney Crowell

recorded by Keith Urban

I'm gonna be here for you, baby. I'll be a man of my word.
Speak the language in a voice that you have never heard.
I wanna sleep with you forever and I wanna die in your arms.
In a cabin by the meadow where the wild bees swarm.

Refrain:
And I'm gonna love you like nobody loves you.
And I'll earn your trust making mem'ries of us.

I wanna honor your mother. And I wanna learn from your pa.
I wanna steal your attention like a bad outlaw.
I wanna stand out in a crowd for you, a man among men.
I wanna make your world better than it's ever been.

Refrain

We'll follow the rainbow wherever the four winds blow.
And there'll be a new day comin' your way.

I'm gonna be here for you from now on, this you know somehow.
You've been stretched to the limits but it's alright now.
I'm gonna make you a promise, if there's life after this,
I'm gonna be there to meet you with a warm wet kiss.

Refrain Twice

Maria Maria

Words and Music by Wyclef Jean, Jerry Duplessis, Carlos Santana, Karl Perazzo, Paul Rekow, Marvin Hough and David McRae

recorded by Santana featuring The Product G&B

Spoken:
Ladies and gents, turn up the sound system
To the sound of Carlos Santana and the G and B.
Ghetto and blues from the refugee gang.

Refrain (sung):
Oh, Maria Maria.
She reminds me of a West Side story.
Growing up in Spanish Harlem
She's living the life just like a movie star.
Oh, Maria, Maria,
She fell in love in East L.A.
To the sounds of the guitar, yeah, yeah,
Played by Carlos Santana.

Stop the looting, stop the shooting,
Pick-pocking on the corner.
See, as the rich is getting richer
The poor is getting poorer.

Se mira Maria on the corner
Thinking of ways to make it better.
In my mailbox there's an eviction letter.
Somebody just said see you later.

Spoken:
Ahora vengo mama chola mama chola.
Ahora vengo mam chola (East coast).
Ahora vengo mama chola mama chola.
Ahora vengo mam chola (West coast).

Refrain

Sung:
I said a la favella los colores.
The streets are getting hotter.
There is no water to put out the fire.
Mi canto la peranza.

Se mira Maria on the corner
Thinking of ways to make it better.
Then I looked up in the sky
Hoping of days of paradise.

Spoken:
Ahora vengo mama chola mama chola.
Ahora vengo mam chola (North side).
Ahora vengo mama chola mama chola.
Ahora vengo mam chola (South side).

Ahora vengo mama chola mama chola.
Ahora vengo mam chola (World wide).
Ahora vengo mama chola mama chola.
Ahora vengo mam chola (Open up your eyes).

Sung:
Maria, you know you're my lover.
When the wind blows I can
Feel you through the weather
And even when we are a part,
Still feels like we're together.

Refrain

Spoken: Put 'em up y'all.
Carlos Santana with the refugee gang.
Wyclef, Jerry "Wonder," Mr. Santana, G and B.
Yo, Carlos man you makin' that guitar cry.

Me Against the Music

Words and Music by Terius Nash, Christopher Stewart, Dorian Hardnett,
Gary O'Brien, Britney Spears, Thabiso Nkhereanye and Madonna Ciccone

recorded by Britney Spears featuring Madonna

All the people in the crowd grab a partner, take it down.

Spoken:
It's me against the music, uh, huh.
It's just me, and me. Yeah. Come on, ooh.
Hey Britney, are you ready? Uh-huh. Are you, uh?

Sung:
And no one cares. It's whippen' my hair,
It's pullin my waist.To hell with stares.
The sweat is drippin' all over my face. And no one's there.
I'm the only one dancin' up in this place. Tonight I'm here.
Feel the beat of the drum, gotta get with that bass.

Refrain:
I'm up against the speaker try'n to take on the music.
It's like a competition, me against the beat.
I wanna get in a zone. I wanna get in a zone.
If you really wanna battle, saddle up and get your rhythm.
Try'n to hit it, chicata. In a minute, I'm a take a you on.
I'm a take a you on, hey, hey, hey.

All my people on the floor,
Let me see you dance. Let me see ya.
All my people wantin' more,
Let me see you dance. I wanna see ya.
All my people round and round,
Let me see you dance. Let me see ya.
All my people in the crowd,
Let me see you dance, I wanna see ya.
How would you like a friendly competition?

Let's take on the song. Let's take on the song
It's you and me, baby, we're the music.
Time to party all night long. All night long.

We're almost there. I'm feelin' it bad
And I can't explain. My soul is bare.
My hips are movin' at a rapid pace.
Baby feel it burn from the tip of my toes,
Runnin' through my veins. And now's your turn.
Let me see what you got, don't hesitate.

Refrain

All my people on the floor,
Let me see you dance. Let me see ya.
All my people wantin' more,
Let me see you dance. I wanna see ya.
All my people round and round,
Let me see you dance. Let me see ya.
All my people in the crowd,
Let me see you dance, I wanna see ya.

Get on the floor. Baby, lose control.
Just work your body and let it go.
If you wanna party just grab somebody.
Hey Britney, we can dance all night long.
Hey Britney, you say you wanna lose control.
Come over here, I got somethin' to show ya.
Sexy lady, I'd rather see you bare your soul.
If you think you're so hot, better show me what you got.
All my people in the crowd, let me see you dance,
Come on Britney, lose control. Grab a partner, take it down.

Get on the floor. Baby, lose control.
Just work your body and let it go.
If you wanna party just grab somebody.
Hey Britney, we can dance all night long.

All my people on the floor,
Let me see you dance. Let me see ya.
All my people wantin' more,
Let me see you dance. I wanna see ya.
All my people round and round,
Let me see you dance. Let me see ya.
All my people in the crowd,
Let me see you dance, I wanna see ya.

All my people in the crowd, let me see you dance.
Come on Briitney, take it down. Make the music dance.
All my people round and round, party all night long.
Come on Britney, lose control. Grab a partner, take it down.

Mr. Brightside

Words and Music by Brandon Flowers, Dave Keuning,
   Mark Stoermer and Ronnie Vannucci

recorded by The Killers

Comin' out of my cage and I've been doin' just fine.
Gotta, gotta be down because I want it all.
It started out with a kiss. How did it end up like this?
It was only a kiss. It was only a kiss.

Now I'm falling asleep and she's calling a cab
While he's having a smoke and she's taking a drag.
Now they're going to bed and my stomach is sick.
And it's all in my head but she's touching his chest now.
He takes off her dress now. Let me go.

I just can't look. It's killing me and taking control.
Jealousy, turning saints into the sea.
Swimming through sick lullabies, choking on your alibis,
But it's just the price I pay. Destiny is calling me.
Open up my eager eyes 'cause I'm Mister Brightside.

I never. I never. I never. I never.

Meant to Live

Words and Music by Jonathan Foreman and Tim Foreman

recorded by Switchfoot

Fumbling his confidence and
Wondering why the world has passed him by.
Hoping that he's bent for more
Than arguments and failed attempt to fly, fly.

Refrain:
We were meant to live for so much more.
Have we lost ourselves?
Somewhere we live inside, somewhere we live inside.
We were meant to live for so much more.
Have we lost ourselves?
Somewhere we live inside.

Dreaming about Providence
And whether mice and men have second tries.
Maybe we've been living with our eyes half open,
Maybe we're bent and broken, broken.

Refrain

We want more than this world's got to offer.
We want more than this world's got to offer.
We want more than the wars of our fathers,
And everything inside screams for second life, yeah!

We were meant to live for so much more.
Have we lost ourselves?
We were meant to live for so much more.
Have we lost ourselves?
We were meant to live for so much more.
Have we lost ourselves?
We were meant to live, we were meant to live.

Miss Independent

Words and Music by Christina Aguilera, Rhett Lawrence, Matthew Morris and Kelly Clarkson

recorded by Kelly Clarkson

Miss Independent. Miss Self Sufficient.
Miss Keep Your Distance.
Miss Unafraid. Miss Out of My Way.
Miss Don't Let A Man Interfere, no.
Miss On Her Own. Miss Almost Grown.
Miss Never Let A Man Help Her Off Her Throne.

So, by keepin' her heart protected
She'd never, never feel rejected.
Little Miss Apprehensive.
Said ooh, she fell in love.

Refrain:
What is this feelin' takin' over?
Thinkin' no one could open the door.
Surprise, it's time to feel what's real.
What happened to Miss Independent?
No longer needs to be defensive.
Goodbye, on you. Real love is true.

Miss Guided Heart. Miss Play It Smart.
Miss If You Wanna Use That Line You Better Not Start, no.
But she miscalculated. She didn't wanna end up jaded
And this Miss decided not to miss out on true love.

So by changin' the misconceptions
She went in a new direction
And found inside she felt a connection.
She fell in love.

Refrain

When Miss Independent walked away,
No time for a love that came her way.
She looked in the mirror and thought today,
What happened to Miss No Longer Afraid?

It took some time for her to see
How beautiful love could truly be.
No more talk of what cannot be real.
I'm so glad I finally feel.

What is the feelin' takin' over?
Thinkin' no one could open the door.
Surprise, it's time to feel what's real.
What happened to Miss Independent?
No longer needs to be defensive.
Goodbye, on you. Real love, real love is true.

Miss Independent.

Missing You

Words and Music by Joshua P. Thompson, Tim Kelley,
  Bob Robinson and Joe Thomas

recorded by Case

Standing here looking out my window,
The nights are long and my days are cold
'Cause I don't have you.
How can I be do damn demanding?
I know you said that it's over now,
But I can't go.
Every day I want to pick up the phone
And tell you that you're everything I need, and more.
If only I could find you.

Refrain:
Like a cold summer afternoon,
Like the snow coming down in June,
Like a wedding without a groom,
I'm missing you.
I'm the desert without the sand.
You're the woman without a man.
I'm the ring without a hand.
I'm missing you.

Driving 'round, thought I saw you pass me.
A rearview mirror's playing tricks on me,
'Cause you fade away.
Maybe I'm just hallucinating,
'Cause my loneliness got the best of me
And my heart's so weak.
Every day I want to pick up the phone
And tell you that you're everything I need, and more.
If only I could find you.

Refrain Twice

Repeat and fade:
Yeah, yeah, yeah, yeah.

A Moment Like This

Words and Music by John Reid and Jorgen Kjell Elofsson

recorded by Kelly Clarkson

What if I told you it was all meant to be?
Would you believe me? Would you agree?
It's almost that feeling we've met before,
So tell me that you don't think I'm crazy
When I tell you love has come here and now.
A moment like this.

Refrain:
Some people wait a lifetime for a moment like this.
Some people search forever for that one special kiss.
Oh, I can't believe it's happening to me.
Some people wait a lifetime for a moment like this.

Everything changes, but beauty remains
Something so tender I can't explain.
Well, I may be dreaming, but still lie awake.
Can't we make this dream last forever?
And I'll cherish all the love we share.
A moment like this.

Refrain

Could this be the greatest love of all?
I wanna know that you will catch me when I fall,
So let me tell you this:
Some people wait a lifetime for a moment like this.

Refrain

Oh, I can't believe it's happening to me.
Some people wait a lifetime for a moment like this,
Oh, like this.

A New Day Has Come

Words and Music by Stephan Moccio and Aldo Nova

recorded by Celine Dion

A new day, ahh. A new day, ahh.

I was waiting for so long
For a miracle to come.
Everyone told me to be strong.
Hold on and don't shed a tear.
Through the darkness and good times
I knew I'd make it through.
And the world thought I had it all
But I was waiting for you.

Hush love, I see a light in the sky.
Oh, it's almost blinding me.
I can't believe I've been
Touched by an angel with love.
Let the rain come down and wash away my tears
Let it fill my soul and drown my fears.
Let it shatter the walls for a new sun.
A new day has come, ahh, oh.

Where it was dark now there's light.
Where there was pain now there's joy.
Where there was weakness I found my strength
All in the eyes of a boy.

Hush love, I see a light in the sky.
Oh, it's almost blinding me.
I can't believe I've been
Touched by an angel with love.
Let the rain come down and wash away my tears
Let it fill my soul and drown my fears.
Let it shatter the walls for a new sun.
A new day has...

Let the rain come down and wash away my tears
Let it fill my soul and drown my fears.
Let it shatter the walls for a new sun.
A new day has come, oh, la, la, oh.
Hush now, I see a light in your eyes,
All in the eyes of a boy.
I can't believe I've been
Touched by a angel with love.
I can't believe I've been
Touched by an angel with love, ooh.

Repeat and Fade:
Hush now, ahh. A new day, ahh.

1985

Words and Music by Mitch Allen, John Allen and Jaret Reddick

recorded by Bowling for Soup

Woo, hoo, hoo. Woo, hoo, hoo.

Debbie just hit the wall. She never had it all.
One prozac a day, husband's a C.P.A.
Her dreams went out the door when she turned twenty-four.
Only been with one man. What happened to her plan?
She was gonna be an actress. She was gonna be a star.
She was gonna shake her ass on the hood of Whitesnake's car.
Her yellow S.U.V. is now the enemy.

Looks like her average life and nothin' has been alright
Since Bruce Springsteen, Madonna. Way before Nirvana
There was U2 and Blondie and music still on MTV.
Her two kids in high school, they tell her that she's uncool.
'Cause she's still preoccupied with nineteen, nineteen,
Nineteen eighty-five.
Woo, hoo, hoo. Nineteen eighty-five. Woo, hoo, hoo.

She's seen all the classics. She knows every line.
Breakfast Club, *Pretty in Pink*, even *St. Elmo's Fire*.
She rocked out to Wham. Not a big Limp Bizkit fan.
Thought she'd get a hand on a member of Duran Duran.
Where's the miniskirt made of snakeskin?
And who's the other guy that's singin' in Van Halen?
When did reality become TV?

Whatever hppened to sitcoms, game shows?
On the radio was Springsteen, Madonna. Way before Nirvana
There was U2 and Blondie and music still on MTV.
Her two kids in high school, they tell her that she's uncool.
'Cause she's still preoccupied with nineteen, nineteen,
Nineteen eighty-five.

She hates time. Make it stop.
When did Motley Crue become classic rock?
And when did Ozzy become an actor?
Please make this stop, stop, stop, and bring back
Springsteen, Madonna. Way before Nirvana
There was U2 and Blondie and music still on MTV.
Her two kids in high school, they tell her that she's uncool.
'Cause she's still preoccupied with nineteen, nineteen,
Nineteen eighty-five.

Bruce Springsteen, Madonna. Way before Nirvana
There was U2 and Blondie and music still on MTV.
Her two kids in high school, they tell her that she's uncool.
'Cause she's still preoccupied with nineteen, nineteen,
Nineteen eighty-five.

Nobody Wants to Be Lonely (Solo Quiero Amarte)

Words and Music by Desmond Child, Victoria Shaw and Gary Burr

recorded by Ricky Martin with Christina Aguilera

Why? Why? Why?

Aqui estoy en mi soledad
Dentro de mi ser solo hay tristeza
Lo he dado todo por salvaar tu amor
Que se va perdiendo necesito tenerte
Quedate junto a mi ven conmigo.

Refrain:
Sin ti me siento tan solo sin ti no puedo mas
Mi cuerpo pide tu cuerpo tu alma acariciar.
Aunque intento yo no puedo encontrar
Si algun secreto se esconde entu piel.
Sin to me siento tan solo
No vivo, porque no puedo amarte.

Why? Why? Why?

Solo tu podras darle la pasion
A mi corazon que no esta latiendo
En tus besos quiero desahogar
Este sentimiento y te busco en mis suenos
Quedate junto a mi, te deseo.

Refrain

Why? Why?

Sabes que estoy muriendo por que te siento lejos
Devuelveme mi pasion todo mi amor,
Mi corazon re gre sa a mi no se vivir,
No, no, no, no. Sin ti me siento tan solo
Sin ti no puedo mas.

Refrain

Why? Why? Why?

Por que no puedo amarte.

Ocean Avenue

Words by Ryan Key
Music by Ryan Key, Sean Mackin, Ben Harper,
   Longineu Parsons III and Peter Mosely

recorded Yellowcard

There's a place off Ocean Avenue
Where I used to sit and talk with you.
We were both sixteen and it felt so right,
Sleepin' all day, stayin' up all night,
Stayin' up all night.

There's a place on the corner of Cherry Street.
We would walk on the beach in our bare feet.
We were both eighteen and it felt so right,
Sleepin' all day, stayin' up all night,
Stayin' up all night.

Refrain:
If I could find you now, things would get better.
We could leave this town and run forever.
Let your waves crash down on me
And take me away, yeah, yeah.

There's a piece of you that's here with me,
It's everywhere I go, it's everything I see.
When I sleep, I dream and it gets me by.
I can make believe that you're here tonight,
That you're here tonight.

Refrain

I remember the look in your eyes
When I told you that this was goodbye.
You were beggin' me, "Not tonight. Not here, not now."
We're lookin' up at the same night sky,
Keep pretendin' the sun will not rise.
We'll be together for one more night somewhere, somehow.

Refrain

On the Way Down

Words and Music by Ryan Cabrera, Curt Frasca and Sabelle Breer

recorded by Ryan Cabrera

Sick and tired of this world.
There's no more air.
Trippin' over myself goin' nowhere.
Waiting, suffocating, no direction.
I took a dive and

Refrain:
On the way down I saw you
And you saved me from myself.
And I won't forget the way you loved me.
And on the way down I almost fell right through
But I held on to you.

I've been wondrin' why it's only me.
Have you always been inside waiting to breathe?
It's all right, sunlight on my face.
I wake up and yeah I'm alive 'cause

Refrain

I was so afraid of goin' under.
But now the weight of the world feels like nothing.
No, nothing. (Down, down, down.)
You're all I wanted. (Down, down, down.)
You're all I needed now. (Down, down, down.)
All I wanted. You're all I needed. Ahh, ahh,
And I won't forget the way you loved me.
Ahh, all that I wanted. All that I needed now.

Refrain

(Down, down, down.) But I held on to you.
(Down, down.) But I held on to you.

100 Years

Words and Music by John Ondrasik

recorded by Five for Fighting

I'm fifteen for a moment,
Caught in between ten and twenty
And I'm just dreaming,
Counting the ways to where you are.

I'm twenty-two for a moment
And she feels better than ever
And we're on fire,
Making our way back from Mars.

Fifteen, there's still time for you.
Time to buy and time to lose.
Fifteen, there's never a wish better than this
When you only got a hundred years to live.

I'm thirty-three for a moment,
I'm still the man, but you see I'm a they;
A kid on the way, a family on my mind.

I'm forty-five for a moment,
The sea is high and I'm heading into a crisis,
Chasing the years of my life.

Fifteen, there's still time for you.
Time to buy and time to lose yourself
Within a morning star.

Fifteen, I'm all right with you.
Fifteen, there's never a wish better than this
When you only got a hundred years to live.

Half time goes by,
Suddenly you're wise,
Another blink of an eye, sixty-seven is gone.
The sun is getting high, we're moving on…

I'm ninety-nine for a moment,
I'm dying for just another moment
And I'm just dreaming,
Counting the ways to where you are.

Fifteen, there's still time for you.
Twenty-two, I feel her too.
Thirty-three, you're on your way.
Every day's a new day…Ooh, ooh, ooh.

Fifteen, there's still time for you.
Time to buy and time to choose.
Hey, fifteen, there's never a wish better than this
When you only got a hundred years to live.

Only Time

Words and Music by Enya, Nicky Ryan and Roma Ryan

from *Sweet November*
recorded by Enya

Who can say where the road goes,
Where the day flows? Only time.
And who can say if your love grows
As your heart chose? Only time.

Refrain:
De da da day. De da da day.
De da day.
De da da da da de. Oh da day.
De da da day da day.

Who can say why your heart sighs,
As your love flies? Only time.
And who can say why your heart cries
When your love lies? Only time.

Refrain

Who can say when the roads meet
That love might be on your heart?
And who can say when the day sleeps
If the night keeps all your heart?
Night keeps all your heart.

De da da day. Da da da day.
De da da day. De da da da oh.

Who can say if your love grows
As your heart chose? Only time.
And who can say where the road goes,
Where the day flows, Only time.

Who know? Only time.
Who knows? Only time.

Out of My Heart (Into Your Head)

Words and Music by Anthony Griffiths, Christopher Griffiths, Christian Burns,
  Mark Barry and Stephen McNally

recorded by BBMak

I feel fine.
Now the rain is gone
And the sun has come to shine.
Nothing can get me down today.

Head over heels.
Got my mind make up
As I'm driving through the fields.
Nothing can get me down again.

Refrain:
Catch me if you can.
I've gotta make a get-a-way.
As the sun goes down waking up my dreams,
And in my mind you're with me once again.
Out of my heart, into your head.
And inside my heart there's a place for you.
And in my mind I'm with you once again.
Out of my heart, into your head.

Chasing the sun.
Tryin' to get away
From the rain that's gonna come.
Hope I can make it all the way.

I'm lost in a crowd.
Tryin' to find my way
But the rain keeps falling down.
Doesn't matter anyway.

Refrain

Take a look at the sky.
Feel the sunshine in your heart.
In your head.
In your own time.

As the sun goes down waking up my dreams,
And in my mind you're with me once again.
Out of my heart, into your head.
And inside my heart there's a place for you.
And in my mind I'm with you once again.
Out of my heart, into your head.
Out of my heart, into your head.
Out of my heart, into your head.

Pieces of Me

Words and Music by Ashlee Simpson, John Shanks and Kara DioGuardi

recorded by Ashlee Simpson

On a Monday I am waiting.
Tuesday, I am fading.
And by Wednesday I can't sleep.
When the phone rings, I hear you.
And the darkness is a clear view
'Cause you won't stop 'til I'm there.
Fall, with you I fall so fast.
I can hardly catch my breath, I hope it lasts.

Ooh, seems like I can finally rest my head
On somethin' real. I like the way that feels.
Ooh, it's as if you know me
Better than I ever knew myself.
I love how you can tell
All the pieces, pieces, pieces of me.
All the pieces, pieces, pieces of me.

I am moody, messy,
I get restless and it's senseless
How you never seem to care.
When I'm angry, you listen.
Make me happy, it's a mission
And you won't stop 'til I'm there.
Fall, with you I fall so fast.
When I hit that bottom crash, you're all I have.

Ooh, seems like I can finally rest my head
On somethin' real. I like the way that feels.
Ooh, it's as if you know me
Better than I ever knew myself.
I love how you can tell
All the pieces, pieces, pieces of me.

How do you know everything I'm about to say?
Am I that obvious?
And if it's written on my face,
I hope it never goes away, yeah.

On a Monday I am waiting.
Tuesday, I am fading into your arms
So I can breathe.

Ooh, seems like I can finally rest my head
On somethin' real. I like the way that feels.
Ooh, it's as if you know me
Better than I ever knew myself.
I love how you can tell.
Ooh, I love how you can tell.
All the pieces, pieces, pieces of me.
All the pieces, pieces, pieces of me.

The Real Slim Shady

Words and Music by Marshall Mathers, Andre Young, Tommy Coster and
Michael Elizondo

Recorded by Eminem

May I have your attention, please?
May I have your attention, please?
Will the real Slim Shady please stand up?
I repeat: will the real Slim Shady please stand up?
We're gonna have a problem here.

Y'all act like you never seen a white person before.
Jaws all on the floor like Pam, like Tommy just burst in the door
And started whoopin' her ass worse than before.
They first were divorce, throwin' her over furniture. (Ahh!)
It the return of the—
(Ah, wait, no way, you're kidding; he didn't just say what I think he
    did, did he?)
And Dr. Dre said…nothing, you idiots.
Dr. Dre's dead; he's locked in my basement! (Ha-ha!)
Feminist women love Eminem. (Chigga, chigga, chigga.)
(Slim Shady—I'm sick of him.
Look at him,
Walkin' around, grabbin' his you-know-what,
Flippin' the you-know-who.)
(Yeah, but he's so cute, though!)
Yeah, I probably got a couple of screws up in my head loose.
But no worse than what's goin' on in your parents' bedrooms.

Sometimes I wanna get on TV and just let loose,
But can't; but it's cool for Tom Greene to hump a dead moose.
(My bum is on your lips; my bum is on your lips.)
And if I'm lucky, you might just give it a little kiss.
And that's the message that we deliver to little kids
And expect them not to know what a woman's clitoris is.
Of course, they gonna know what intercourse is
By the time they hit fourth grade.
The got the Discovery Channel, don't they?
(We ain't nothin' but mammals.)
Well, some of us cannibals
Who cut other people open like cantaloupes. (Slurp.)
But if we can hump dead animals and antelopes
Then there's no reason that a man and another man can't elope.
   (Eww!)
But if you feel like I feel, I got the antidote.
Women, wave your pantyhose;
Sing the chorus, and it goes—

Refrain:
I'm Slim Shady, yes, I'm the real Shady.
All you other Slim Shadys are just imitating.
So won't the real Slim Shady please stand up,
Please stand up, please stand up?
I'm Slim Shady, yes, I'm the real Shady.
All you other Slim Shadys are just imitating.
So won't the real Slim Shady please stand up,
Please stand up, please stand up?

Will Smith don't gotta cuss in his raps to sell his records.
Well, I do—so fuck him and fuck you, too!
You think I give a damn about a Grammy?
Half of you critics can't even stomach me, let alone stand me.
(But Slim, what if you win; wouldn't it be weird?)
Why? So you guys could just lie to get me here?
So you can sit me here, next to Britney Spears?
Shit, Christina Aguilera better switch me chairs
So I can sit next to Carson Daly and Fred Durst
And hear 'em argue over who she gave head to first.
You little bitch, put me on, blast on MTV.
(Yeah, he's cute, but I think he's married to Kim, he-he!)
I should download her audio on MP3
And show the whole world how you gave Eminem V.D. (Ahh!)
I'm sick of you little-girl and -boy groups—all you do is annoy me.
So I have been sent here to destroy you; (Bzzzt.)
And there's a million of us just like me,
Who cuss like me; who just don't give a fuck like me;
Who dress like me; walk, talk, and act like me;
And just might be the next best thing, but not quite me!

Refrain

I'm like a head-trip to listen to 'cause I'm only givin' you
Things you joke about with your friends inside your living room.
The only difference is I got the balls to say it
In front of y'all, and I don't gotta be false or sugar-coated at all—
I just get on the mic and spit it.
And whether you like to admit it,
Er, I just shit it
Better than ninety percent of you rappers out there can.
Then you wonder, "How can kids eat up these albums like Valiums?"

It's funny 'cause at the rate I'm goin', when I'm thirty
I'll be the only person in the nursing home flirtin',
Pinchin' nurses' asses when I'm jacking-off with Jergens,
And I'm jerkin', but this whole bag of Viagra isn't workin',
And every single person is a Slim Shady, lurkin'.
He could be workin' at Burger King,
Spittin' on your onion rings, (Hach.)
Or in the parking lot, circling,
Screamin', "I don't give a fuck!"
With his windows down and his system up.
So, will the real Slim Shady please stand up
And put one of those fingers on each hand up?
And be proud to be outta your mind and outta control,
And one more time, loud as you can—how does it go?

Refrain Twice

Ha-ha!
Guess there's a Slim Shady in all of us.
Fuck it—let's all stand up.

Redneck Woman

Words and Music by Gretchen Wilson and John Rich

recorded by Gretchen Wilson

Well, I ain't never been the Barbie Doll type.
No, I can't swig that sweet champagne;
I'd rather drink beer all night in a tavern
Or in a honky-tonk or on a four wheel drive tailgate.
I got posters on my wall of Skynyrd, Kid and Strait.
Some people look down on me, but I don't give a rip.
I stand barefooted in my own front yard
With a baby on my hip 'cause

I'm a redneck woman, I ain't no high class broad.
I'm just a product of my raisin', I say, "Hey y'all" and "Hee-haw."
And I keep my Christmas lights on, on my front porch all year long
And I know all the words to every Charlie Daniels song.
So, here's to all my sisters out there keepin' it country.
Let me get a big "Hell yeah" from the redneck girls like me.
Hell, yeah. (Hell yeah!)

Victoria's Secret, well, their stuff's real nice,
Woah, but I can buy the same damn thing
On a Wal Mart shelf half price and still look sexy,
Just as sexy as those models on T.V.
No, I don't need no designer's tag to make my man want me.
You might think I'm trashy, a little too hardcore,
But in my neck of the woods, I'm just the girl next door.

Hey, I'm a redneck woman, I ain't no high class broad.
I'm just a product of my raisin', I say, "Hey y'all" and "Hee-haw."
And I keep my Christmas lights on, on my front porch all year long
And I know all the words to every Tanya Tucker song.
So, here's to all my sisters out there keepin' it country.
Let me get a big "Hell yeah" from the redneck girls like me.
Hell, yeah. (Hell yeah!)

I'm a redneck woman, I ain't no high class broad.
I'm just a product of my raisin', I say, "Hey y'all" and "Hee-haw."
And I keep my Christmas lights on, on my front porch all year long
And I know all the words to every ol' Bosephus song.
So, here's to all my sisters out there keepin' it country.
Let me get a big "Hell yeah" from the redneck girls like me.
(Hell, yeah!) Hell yeah! (Hell, yeah!) Hell yeah!
(Hell, yeah!) I said, hell yeah!

Rock Your Body

Words and Music by Pharrell Williams, Chad Hugo and Justin Timberlake

recorded by Justin Timberlake

Refrain:
Don't be so quick to walk away.
Dance with me. I wanna rock your body.
Please stay. Dance with me.
You don't have to admit you wanna play.
Dance with me.
Just let me rock you 'til the break of day.
Dance with me.

Got time, but I don't mind.
Just wanna rock you, girl. I'll have whatever you had.
Come on, let's give it a whirl.
See, I been watchin' you and I like the way you move.
So go 'head girl, just do that ass-shakin' thing you do.

So you grab your girls, and you grab a couple more
And you all can meet me in the middle of the floor.
Said the air it thick, it's smellin' right,
So you pass to the left and you sail to the right.

Refrain

I don't mean you no harm, just wanna rock you girl.
You can move, but be calm. Let's go, let's give it a whirl.
See, it appears to me you like the way I move.
I tell you what I'm gon' do: pull you close and share my groove.

So you grab your girls, and you grab a couple more
And you all can meet me tin the middle of the floor.
Said the air it thick, it's smellin' right,
So you pass to the left and you sail to the right.

Refrain

Talk to me, boy.
No disrespect. I don't mean no harm.
Talk to me, boy.
I can't wait to have you in my arms.
Talk to me, boy.
Hurry up, 'cause you talkin' too long.
Talk to me boy.
Better have you naked by the end of this song.

So what did you come here for?
(I came to dance with you)
I know that you don't wanna hit the floor.
(Make some romance with you.)
You been searchin' for love forever more
(And I'll take a chance…)
If love is here on the floor, girl.
Hey, dance with me, yeah.

Refrain

Talk to me, boy.
No disrespect. I don't mean no harm.
Talk to me, boy.
I can't wait to have you in my arms.
Talk to me, boy.
Hurry up, 'cause you talkin' too long.
Talk to me boy.
Better have you naked by the end of this song.

Poomts, poomts, poomah, ah-ah,
Ah-poomts poom, poom di poom, shot.
Poomts, poomts, poomah, ah-ah,
Ah-poomts poom, poom di poom, shot.

Poomts, poomts, poomah, ah-ah,
Ah-poomts poom, poom di poom, shot.
Poomts, poomts, poomah, ah-ah,
Ah-poomts poom, poom di poom, shot.

Don't be so quick to walk away.
Spoken: Just thinkin' of you.
I like the way you look right now.
Sung: Don't be so quick to walk away.
Don't be so quick to walk away
Spoken: Come over here, baby.

Sung: Poomts, poomts, poomah, ah-ah,
Ah-poomts poom, poom di poom,
Spoken: Let's make the bed, 'cause I…
Poomts, poomts, poomah, ah-ah,
Ah-poomts poom, poom di poom,
Spoken: Are you feelin me?

Let's do somethin'.
I better have you naked by the end of this song.

The Way You Move

Words and Music by Antwan Patton, Patrick Brown and Carlton Mahone

recorded by Outkast featuring Sleepy Brown

Boom, boom, boom, hah, hah.

Rap 1:
Ready for action, nip it in the bud.
Whenever relaxin'. OutKast is everlastin'.
Not clashin', not at all.
But see, my nigga went up to do a little actin'.
Now that's for anyone askin'.
Give me one, pass 'em.
Drip, drip, drop, there goes an eargasm.
Now you comin' out the side of your face.
We tappin' right into your memory banks, thanks.
So click it or ticket, let's see your seatbelt fastened.
Trunk rattlin' like two midgets in the back seat wrestlin'
Speakerboxxx vibrate the tag.
Make it sound like aluminum cans in the bag.
But I know y'all wanted that eight-o-eight.
Can you feel that B-A-S-S, bass?
But I know y'all wanted that eight-o-eight.
Can you feel that B-A-S-S, bass?

I like the way you move. I like the way you move.
Woo, I love the way you move.
I love the way. I love the way.
I love the way you love. I love the way you move.
Woo, I love the way you move.
I love the way. I love the way.

Rap 2:
The whole room fell silent. The girls all paused with glee.
Turnin' left, turnin' right, are they lookin' at me?
Well I was lookin' at them, there, there on the dance floor.
Now they got me in the middle feelin' like a man whore.
Especially the big girl. Big girls need love too.
No discrimination here, squirrel. So keep your hands off my cheeks.
Let me study how you ride the beat, you big freak.
Skinny slim women got the camel-toe within' 'em.
You can hump them, lift them, bend them,
Give them something to remember.
Yell out "timber" when you fall through the chop shop.
Take a deep breath and exhale.
Your ex-male friend, boyfriend was boring as hell.
Will let me listen to the story you tell.
And we can make moves like a person in jail…
On the low, hoe!

I like the way you move. I like the way you move.
Woo, I love the way you move.
I love the way. I love the way.
I love the way you love. I love the way you move.
Woo, I love the way you move.
I love the way. I love the way.

Hey baby, girl don't you stop it.
Come on lady, dance all around me.
You look so fine, look so fine.
Look so fine, drivin' me out of my mind, out of my mind.
If I could, I would just leave with you baby.
Ooh, 'cause you light me, and excite me.
And you know you got me baby.

Repeat and Fade:
I like the way you move. I like the way you move.
Woo, I love the way you move.
I love the way. I love the way.
I love the way you love. I love the way you move.
Woo, I love the way you move.
I love the way. I love the way.

Shape of My Heart

Words and Music by Martin Sandberg, Rami Yacoub and Lisa Miskovsky

recorded by Backstreet Boys

Mm, mm, yeah, yeah.

Baby, please try to forgive me.
Stay here, don't put out the glow.
Hold me now, don't bother
If ev'ry minute makes me weaker,
You can save me from the man that I've become.
Oh, yeah.

Refrain:
Looking back on the things I've done,
I was trying to be someone.
I played my part and kept you in the dark.
Now let me show you the shape of my heart.

Sadness is beautiful. Loneliness is tragical.
So help me, I can't win the war, oh, no.
Touch me now, don't bother
If every second makes me weaker,
You can save me from the man that I've become.
Oh yeah.

Refrain

I'm here with my confession,
Got nothing to hide no more.
I don't know where to start
But to show you the shape of my heart.

Refrain Twice

Looking back on the things I've done,
I was trying to be someone.
I played my part and kept you in the dark.
Now let me show you the shape of,
Show you the shape of my heart.

She Bangs

Words and Music by Desmond Child, Walter Afanasieff and Robi Rosa

recorded by Ricky Martin

Talk to me, tell me your name.
You blow me off like it's all the same.
You lit a fuse and now I'm
Tickin' away like a bomb, yeah baby.

Talk to me, tell me your sign.
You're switchin' sides like a Gemini.
You're playing games and now you're
Hittin' my heart like a drum, yeah baby.

Well if Lady Luck gets on my side
We're gonna rock this town alive.
I'll let her rough me up 'til she knocks me out,
'Cause she walks like she talks
And she talks like she walks.

Refrain:
She bangs, she bangs.
Oh baby, when she moves, she moves.
I go crazy 'cause she looks like a flower
But she stings like a bee
Like every girl in history.
She bangs, she bangs.
I'm wasted by the way she moves, she moves.
No one ever looked so fine.
She reminds me that a woman's got
One thing on her mind.

Talk to me, tell me your name.
I'm just a link in your daisy chain.
Your rap sounds like a diamond map
To the stars, yeah baby.

Talk to me, tell me the news.
You wear me out like pair of shoes.
We'll dance until the band goes home
Then you're gone, yeah baby.

Well, if it looks like love should be a crime,
You better lock me up for life.
I'll do the time with a smile on my face,
Thinking of her in her leather and lace.

Refrain

And if Lady Luck gets on my side
We're gonna rock this town alive.
I'll let her rough me up 'til she knocks me out,
'Cause she walks like she talks
And she talks like she walks.

She bangs, she bangs.
Oh baby, when she moves, she moves.
I go crazy 'cause she looks like a flower
But she stings like a bee
Like every girl in history.

Repeat and Fade:
She bangs, she bangs.
Ooh, she moves, she moves.
Ooh, ooh, ooh, oh, oh, oh.

She Will Be Loved

Words and Music by Adam Levine and James Valentine

recorded by Maroon5

Beauty queen of only eighteen.
She had some trouble with herself.
He was always there to help her.
She always belonged to someone else.

I drove for miles and miles
And wound up at your door.
I've had you so many times
But somehow I want more.

Refrain:
I don't mind spending every day
Out on your corner in the pouring rain.
Look for the girl with the broken smile.
Ask her if she wants to stay a while
And she will be loved. And she will be loved.

Tap on my window, knock on my door.
I want to make you feel beautiful.
I know I tend to get so insecure.
Doesn't matter anymore.

It's not always rainbows and butterflies.
It's compromise that moves us along, yeah.
My heart is full and my door's always open.
You come anytime you want, yeah.

Refrain

And she will be loved. And she will be loved.

I know where you hide alone in your car.
Know all of the things that make you who you are.
I know that goodbye means nothing at all.
Comes back and begs me,
Catch her every time she falls, yeah.

Tap on my window, knock on my door.
I want to make you feel beautiful.

Refrain

And she will be loved. And she will be loved.
Please don't try so hard to say goodbye.
Please don't try so hard to say goodbye.
Please don't try so hard to say goodbye.

So Yesterday

Words and Music by Graham Edwards, Scott Spock, Lauren Christy
and Charlie Midnight

recorded by Hilary Duff

So yesterday, so yesterday, so yesterday.

You can change your life if you wanna.
You can change your clothes if you wanna.
If you change your mind well that's the way it goes.
But I'm gonna keep your jeans
And your old black hat 'cause I wanna.
They look good on me.
You're never gonna get them back,
At least not today, not today, not today.

Refrain:
'Cause it it's over let it go and come tomorrow
It will seem so yesterday, so yesterday.
I'm just a bird that's already flown away.
Laugh it off and let it go and when you wake up
It will seem so yesterday, so yesterday.
Haven't you heard that I'm gonna be okay?

Okay, you can say you're bored if you wanna.
You could act real tough if you wanna.
You could say you're torn but I've heard enough.
Thank you. You made my mind up for me
When you started to ignore me.
Do you see a single tear?
It isn't gonna happen here,
At least not today, not today, not today.

Refrain

If you're over me, I'm already over you.
If it's all been done, what is left to do?
How can you hang up if the line is dead?
If you wanna walk, I'm a step ahead.
If you're movin' on, I'm already gone.
If the light is off, then it isn't on,
At least not today, not today, not today.

'Cause it it's over let it go and come tomorrow
It will seem so yesterday, so yesterday.
I'm just a bird that's already flown away.
Laugh it off and let it go and when you wake up
It will seem so yesterday, so yesterday.
Haven't you heard?

Refrain

Soak Up the Sun

Words and Music by Jeff Trott and Sheryl Crow

recorded by Sheryl Crow

My friend the communist
Holds meetings in his R.V.
I can't afford his gas
So I'm stuck here watching T.V.
I don't have digital.
I don't have diddly squat.
It's not having what you want.
It's wanting what you've got.

Refrain:
I'm gonna soak up the sun.
I'm gonna tell everyone to lighten up.
I'm gonna tell 'em that I've got no one to blame.
But every time I feel lame I'm lookin' up.

I'm gonna soak up the sun.
I'm gonna soak up the sun.

I've got a crummy job.
It don't pay near enough
To buy the things it'd take
To win me some of you love.
Every time I turn around
I'm lookin' up you're lookin' down.
Maybe something's wrong with you
That makes you act the way you do.

Refrain

I'm gonna soak up the sun
While it's still free.
I'm gonna soak up the sun
Before it goes out on me.
Doesn't have no master suite
But I'm still the king of me.
You have a fancy ride but baby,
I'm the one who has the key.

Every time I turn around
I'm lookin' up, you're lookin' down.
Maybe something's wrong with you
That makes you act the way you do.
Maybe I am crazy too.

Refrain Twice

I, I'm gonna soak up the sun.
I've got my forty-five on so I can rock on.

Somebody Told Me

Words and Music by Brandon Flowers, Dave Keuning,
   Mark Stoermer and Ronnie Vannucci

recorded by The Killers

Breakin' my back just to know your name.
Seventeen tracks and I've had it with this game.
I'm breakin' my back just to know your name.
But heaven ain't close in a place like this.
Anything goes but don't blink you might miss.

'Cause heaven ain't close in a place like this.
I said a heaven ain't close in a place like this.
Bring it back down.
Bring it back down tonight, hoo, hoo.

Never thought I'd let a rumor ruin my moonlight.
Well, somebody told me you had a boyfriend
Who looks like a girlfriend
That I had in February of last year.
It's not confidential. I've got potential.

Ready, let's roll onto something new.
Takin' its toll then I'm leaving without you.
'Cause heaven ain't close in a place like this.
I said a heaven ain't close in a place like this.
Bring it back down.
Bring it back down tonight, hoo, hoo.

Never thought I'd let a rumor ruin my moonlight.
Well, somebody told me you had a boyfriend
Who looks like a girlfriend
That I had in February of last year.
It's not confidential. I've got potential
A-rushing, a-rushing around.

Pace yourself for me, I said maybe, baby, please.
But I just don't know now.
Maybe, baby, when all I wanna do is try.
Well, somebody told me you had a boyfriend
Who looks like a girlfriend
That I had in February of last year.
It's not confidential. I've got potential
A-rushing, a-rushing around.

Now somebody told me you had a boyfriend
Who looks like a girlfriend
That I had in February of last year.
It's not confidential. I've got potential
A-rushing, a-rushing around.

The Space Between

Words and Music by David J. Matthews and Glen Ballard

recorded by Dave Matthews Band

You cannot quit me so quickly.
Is no hope in you for me.
No corner you could squeeze me,
But I got all the time for you, love.

The space between the tears we cry
Is the laughter keeps us coming back for more.
The space between the wicked lies
We tell and hope to keep us safe from the pain.

But will I hold you again?
These fickle, fuddled words confuse me,
Like, will it rain today?
We waste the hours with talking, talking,
These twisted games we're playing.

We're strange allies with warring hearts.
What a wild eyed beast you be.
The space between the wicked lies
We tell and hope to keep us safe from the pain.

But will I hold you again? Will I hold...

Look at us spinning out
In the madness of a roller coaster.
You know you went off like the devil
In a church in the middle of a crowded room.
All I can do, my love,
Is hope we don't take this ship down.

The space between where you smile and hide
Is where you'll find me if I get to go.
The space between the bullets in our firefight
Is where I'll be hiding, waiting for you.

The rain that falls splashed in your heart,
Ran like sadness down the window into your room.
The space between our wicked lies is where
We hope to keep safe from pain.
Take my hand 'cause we're walking out of here.
Oh, right out of here. Love is all we need, dear.

The space between what's wrong and right
Is where you'll find me hiding, waiting for you.
The space between your heart and mine
Is the space we'll fill with time.
The space between…

Stacy's Mom

Words and Music by Chris Collingwood and Adam Schlesinger

recorded by Fountains of Wayne

Stacy's mom has got it going on.
Stacy's mom has got it going on.
Stacy's mom has got it going on.
Stacy's mom has got it going on.

Stacy, can I come over after school?
(After school?)
We can hang around by the p-p-p-pool.
(Hang by the pool.)
Did your mom get back from her business trip?
(Business trip?)
Is she there, or is she tryin' to give me the slip?
(Give me the slip?)
You know I'm not the little boy that I used to be.
I'm all grown up now, baby, can't you see?

Refrain:
Stacy's mom has got it going on.
She's all I want and I've waited for so long.
Stacy, can't you see you're not the girl for me?
I know it might be wrong
But I'm in love with Stacy's mom.

Stacy's mom has got it going on.
Stacy's mom has got it going on.

Stacy, do you remember when I mowed your lawn?
(Mowed your lawn?)
Your mom came out with just a towel on.
(Towel on.)
I could tell she liked me from the way she stared.
(Way she stared.)
And the way, she said, "You missed a spot over there."
(Spot over there.)
And I know that you think it's just a fantasy,
But since your dad walked out,
Your mom could use a guy like me.

Refrain Twice

Ahh, ahh, I'm in love with Stacy's mom.
Ahh, ahh, wait a minute.
Stacy, can't you see you're just not the girl for me?
I know it might be wrong
But I'm in love with Stacy's mom.

Superman (It's Not Easy)

Words and Music by John Ondrasik

recorded by Five For Fighting

I can't stand to fly.
I'm not that naïve.
I'm just out to find
The better part of me.

I'm more than a bird.
I'm more than a plane.
I'm more than some pretty face beside a train.

And it's not easy to be me.
I wish that I could cry,
Fall upon my knees,
Find a way to lie
'Bout a home I'll never see.

It may sound absurd,
But don't be naïve.
Even heroes have the right to bleed.

I may be disturbed,
But won't you concede
Even heroes have the right to dream?
And it's not easy to be me.

Up, up and away, away from me.
Well it's alright, you can all sleep sound tonight.
I'm not crazy or anything.

I can't stand to fly.
I'm not that naïve.
Men weren't meant to ride
With clouds between their knees.

I'm only a man
In a silly red sheet,
Digging for kryptonite on this one-way street.

Only a man
In a silly red sheet
Looking for special things inside of me,

Inside of me, inside of me.
Yeah, inside of me, inside of me.

I'm only a man
In a funny red sheet.
I'm only a man looking for a dream.

I'm only a man
In a funny red sheet
And it's not easy, ooh, ooh, ooh.
It's not easy to be me.

Take Me Out

Words and Music by Alex Kapranos and Nick McCarthy

recorded by Franz Ferdinand

So if you're lonely,
You know I'm here waiting for you.
I'm just a crosshair
I'm just a shot away from you.

And if you leave here,
You leave me broken, shattered I lie.
I'm just a crosshair
I'm just a shot, then we can die.

Aah, I know I won't be leaving here with you.

I say don't you know?
You say you don't know.
I say take me out
I say you don't show,
Don't move time is slow.
I say take me out.

I say you don't know?
You say you don't know.
I say take me out
If I move things could die,
If eyes move, this could die.
I want you to take me out.

I know I won't be leaving here,
Oh, I know I won't be leaving here.
I know I won't be leaving here,
Oh, I know I won't be leaving here, with you.

I say don't you know?
You say you don't know.
I say take me out
If I wink, this could die,
If I blink, this could die.
I want you to take me out.

If I move this could die,
If eyes move this can die.
Come on, take me out.
I know I won't be leaving here,
Oh, I know I won't be leaving here.
I know I won't be leaving here,
Oh, I know I won't be leaving here, with you.

Thank You

Words and Music by Paul Herman and Dido Armstrong

recorded by Dido

My tea's gone cold; I'm wondering why
I got out of bed at all.
The morning rain clouds up my window
And I can't see at all,
And even if I could it'd all be grey,
But your pictures on my wall,
It reminds me that it's not so bad,
It's not so bad.

I drank too much last night, got bills to pay.
My head just feels in pain.
I missed the bus and there'll be hell today;
I'm late for work again.
And even if I'm there they'll all imply
That I might not last the day,
And then you call me and it's not so bad,
It's not so bad.

Refrain:
And I want to thank you
For giving me the best day of my life.
And oh, just to be with you
Is having the best day of my life.

Push the door; I'm home at last,
And I'm soaking through and through.
And then you handed me a towel,
And all I see is you.
And even if my house falls down now,
I wouldn't have a clue,
Because you're near me.

Refrain Twice

There You'll Be

Words and Music by Diane Warren

from Touchstone Pictures'/Jerry Bruckheimer Films' *Pearl Harbor*
recorded by Faith Hill

When I think back on these times
And the dreams we left behind,
I'll be glad, 'cause I was blessed to get,
To have you in my life.
When I think back on these days
I'll look and see your face.
You were right there for me.

In my dreams I'll always see
You soar above the sky.
In my heart there'll always be
A place for you, for all my life.
I'll keep a part of you with me,
And everywhere I am, there you'll be,
And everywhere I am, there you'll be.

Well, you showed me how it feels
To feel the sky within my reach,
And I always will remember
All the strength you gave to me.
Your love made me make it through;
Oh, I owe so much to you.
You were right there for me.

In my dreams I'll always see
You soar above the sky.
In my heart there'll always be
A place for you, for all my life.
I'll keep a part of you with me,
And everywhere I am, there you'll be.

'Cause I always saw in you my light, my strength,
And I wanna thank you now for all the ways
You were right there for me.
You were right there for me, for always.

In my dreams I'll always see
You soar above the sky.
In my heart there'll always be
A place for you, for all my life.
I'll keep a part of you with me,
And everywhere I am, there you'll be,
And everywhere I am, there you'll be.
There you'll be.

This Is the Night

Words and Music by Gary Burr, Aldo Nova and Christopher Braide

recorded by Clay Aiken

When the world wasn't upside down,
I could take all the time I had.
But I'm not gonna wait
When a moment can vanish so fast.
'Cause every kiss is a kiss
You can never get back.

Lift me up in your eyes.
If you told me that is what Heaven is,
Well, you'd be right.
I've been waiting forever for this,
This is the night.

When the answer to all my dreams
Is as close as a touch away,
Why am I here holdin' back
What I'm trying to say?

Lift me up in your eyes.
If you told me that is what heaven is,
Well, you'd be right.
Hold me close to your heart.
I would go with you to the ends
Of the earth, and we'll fly.
I've been waiting forever for this,
This is the night.

This is the night where we capture forever
And all our tomorrows begin.
After tonight we will never be lonely again.

Lift me up in your eyes.
If you told me that is what heaven is,
Well, you'd be right.
Hold me close to your heart.
I would go with you to the ends
Of the earth, and we'll fly.
I've been waiting forever for this,
This is the night.

This Love

Words and Music by Adam Levine and Jesse Carmichael

recorded by Maroon5

I was so high I did not recognize
The fire burning in her eyes.
The chaos that controlled my mind.
I whispered goodbye, she got on a plane
Never to return again.
But always in my heart, oh.

Refrain:
This love has taken its toll on me.
She said goodbye too many times before.
And her heart is breaking in front of me.
And I have no choice 'cause
I won't say goodbye anymore.

I tried my best to feed her appetite,
Keep her coming every night.
So hard to keep her satisfied.
Kept playing love like it was just a game.
Pretending to feel the same
Then turn around and leave again, but oh.

Refrain

I'll fix these broken things.
Repair your broken wings
And make sure everything's alright. It's alright.
My pressure on your hips.
Sinking my fingertips to every inch of you
Because I know that's what you want me to do.

Refrain

This love has taken its toll on me.
She said goodbye too many times before.
And my heart is breaking in front of me.
She said goodbye too many times before.

Refrain Twice

A Thousand Miles

Words and Music by Vanessa Carlton

recorded by Vanessa Carlton

Making my way downtown, walking fast.
Faces pass and I'm homebound.
Staring blankly ahead, just making my way,
Making a way through the crowd.

Refrain:
And I need you and I'll miss you,
And now I wonder, if I could fall into the sky,
Do you think time would pass me by?
'Cause you know I'd walk a thousand miles
If I could just see you tonight.

It's always times like these when I think of you
And I wonder if you ever think of me.
'Cause everything's so wrong and I don't belong
Living in your precious memory.

Refrain

And I, I don't want to let you know.
I, I drown in your memory.
I, I don't want to let this go.
I, I don't.

Making my way downtown, walking fast.
Faces pass and I'm homebound.
Staring blankly ahead, just making my way,
Making a way through the crowd.

And I need you and I'll miss you,
And now I wonder, if I could fall into the sky,
Do you think time would pass me by?
'Cause you know I'd walk a thousand miles
If I could just see you.

If I could fall into the sky,
Do you think time would pass me by?
'Cause you know I'd walk a thousand miles
If I could just see you,
If I could just hold you tonight.

True

Words and Music by Ryan Cabrera, Jimmy Harry and Sheppard Solomon

recorded by Ryan Cabrera

I won't talk. I won't breathe.
I won't move 'til you finally see
That you belong with me.

You might think I don't look
But deep inside the corner of my mind
I'm attached to you.
Umm, I'm weak, it's true,
'Cause I'm afraid to know the answer.
Do you want me too?
'Cause my heart keeps falling faster.

I've waited all my life to cross this line
To the only thing that's true.
So I will not hide. It's time to try
Anything to be with you.
All my life I've waited, this is true.

You don't know what you do
Every time you walk into the room
I'm afraid to move.
I'm weak, it's true,
I'm just scared to know the ending.
Do you see me too?
Do you even know you met me?

Refrain

I know when I go,
I'll be on my way to you.
The way that's true.

Refrain

Underneath It All

Words and Music by David A. Stewart and Gwen Stefani

recorded by No Doubt

It's times when I want someone more,
A-someone more like me,
And there's times when this dress rehearsal
Seems incomplete, but
You see the colors in me like no one else
And behind your dark glasses you're,
You're something else.

Refrain:
And you're really lovely underneath it all,
And you want to love me underneath it all.
I'm really lucky underneath it all,
And you're really lovely.

You know some real bad tricks
And you need some discipline,
But lately you've been trying real hard
And giving me your best,
And you give me the most gorgeous sleep
That I've ever had, and when it's really bad,
I guess it's not that bad.

Refrain

It's so many moons that we have seen
A-stumbling back next to me.
I've seen right through and underneath,
And you make me better.
I've seen right through and underneath,
And you make me better, better, better.

For real, 'cause underneath it all,
You are my real Prince Charming.
Like the heat from the fire
You were always burning.
Anytime you're around
My body keeps calling for your touch,
Your kisses and your sweet romancing.

There's another side of you a-dis a-woman here adore.
Aside from your temper everything else secure.
You're good for me baby; of that I'm sure,
'Cause over and over and over again I want more.
You've used up all your coupons
And all you've got left is me,
And somehow I'm full of forgiveness;
I guess it's meant to be.

Refrain Twice

Mm, mm, mm, underneath it all.

Underneath Your Clothes

Words and Music by Shakira
Music co-written by Lester A. Mendez

recorded by Shakira

You're a song written by the hands of God.
Don't get me wrong 'cause this might sound to you a bit odd.
But you won the place where all my thought go hiding.
Right under your clothes is where I'll find them.

Refrain:
Underneath your clothes there's an endless story.
There's the man I chose.
There's my territory and all the things I deserve
For being such a good girl, honey.

'Cause of you, I forgot the smart ways to lie.
Because of you I'm running out of reasons to cry.
When the friends are gone, when the party's over,
We will still belong to each other.

Refrain

Underneath your clothes there's an endless story.
There's the man I chose.
There's my territory and all the things I deserve
For being such a-a-a-a-a...

I love you more than all that's on the planet
Movin', walkin', talkin', breathin'.
You know it's true, oh babe,
It's so funny you almost don't believe it.

As every voice is hangin' from the silence,
Lights are hangin' from the ceiling.
Like a lady tied to her manners,
I'm tied up to this feeling.

Refrain

Underneath you clothes, ooh.
There's the man I chose.
There's my territory and all the things I deserve
For being such a good girl,
For being such a good girl.

Wasting My Time

Words and Music by Danny Craig, Dallas Smith, Jeremy Hora and Dave Benedict

recorded by Default

I don't want to see you waiting.
I've already gone too far away.
I still can't keep the day from ending.
No more messed up reasons for me to stay.

Well, this is not for real, afraid to feel
I just hit the floor, don't ask for more.
I'm wasting my time. I'm wasting my time.
Can't you stop the feeling? There is no reason.
Just make the call and take it all again, oh, again.

Months went by with us pretending.
When did our light turn from green to red?
I took a chance and left you standing.
Lost the will to do this once again.

Well, this is not for real, afraid to feel
I just hit the floor, don't ask for more.
I'm wasting my time. I'm wasting my time.
Can't you drop the feeling? There is no reason.
Just make the call and take it all I'm wasting my time.
I'm wasting my time again, oh again.

I see you waiting. Look so lonely.
I see you waiting. I see you waiting.

Well, this is not for real, afraid to feel
I just hit the floor, don't ask for more.
I'm wasting my time. I'm wasting my time.
Can't you stop the feeling? There is no reason.
Just make the call and take it all I'm wasting my time.
I'm wasting my,

Well, this is not for real, afraid to feel
I just hit the floor, don't ask for more.
I'm wasting my time. I'm wasting my time.
You can't stop the feeling. There is no reason.
Just make the call and take it all again, whoa again.

We Belong Together

Words and Music by Mariah Carey, Jermaine Dupri, Manuel Seal, Johnta Austin,
 Darnell Bristol, Kenneth Edmonds, Sidney Johnson, Patrick Moten,
 Bobby Womack and Sandra Sully

recorded by Mariah Carey

Ah, oh, sweet love.

I didn't mean it when I said I didn't love you so.
I should have held on tight, I never should've let you go.
I didn't know nothing. I was stupid.
I was foolish. I was lyin' to myself.
I could not fathom that I would ever be without your love.
Never imagined I'd be sitting here beside myself.
Guess I didn't know you, guess I didn't know me.
But I thought I knew everything.
I never felt the feeling that I'm feeling
Now that I don't hear your voice
Or have your touch and kiss your lips
'Cause I don't have a choice. Oh what I wouldn't give
To have you lying by my side right here.

Refrain:
'Cause baby, when you left I lost a part of me.
It's still so hard to believe.
Come back, baby, please, 'cause we belong together.
Who else am I gonna lean on when times get rough?
Who's gonna talk to me on the phone till the sun comes up?
Who's gonna take your place? There ain't nobody better.
Oh, baby, baby, we belong together.

I can't sleep at night when you are on my mind.
Bobby Womack's on the radio singin' to me,
"If you think you're lonely now."
Wait a minute, this is too deep, too deep.
I gotta change the station.
So I turn the dial, tryin' to catch a break.
And then I hear Babyface. "I only think of you"
And it's breaking my heart.
I'm tryin' to keep it together but I'm falling apart.
I'm feeling all out of my element.
Throwing things, crying,
Tryin' to figure out where the hell I went wrong.
The pain reflected in this song
Ain't even half of what I'm feeling inside.
I need you, need you back in my life.

Refrain Twice

Repeat and fade:
Ooo, yeah. Ooo, yeah.

When I'm Gone

Words and Music by Matt Roberts, Brad Arnold, Christopher Henderson and
  Robert Harrell

recorded by 3 Doors Down

There's another world inside of me
That you may never see.
There's secrets in this life that I can't hide.
Well, somewhere in this darkness,
There's a light that I can't find.
Well, maybe it's too far away, yeah,
Or maybe I'm just blind.
Yeah, maybe I'm just blind.

Refrain:
So, hold me when I'm here.
Right me when I'm wrong.
Hold me when I'm scared
And love me when I'm gone.
Everything I am and everything in me
Wants to be the one you wanted me to be.
I'll never let you down, even if I could.
I'd give up everything if only for your good.
So, hold me when I'm here.
Right me when I'm wrong.
You can hold me when I'm scared.
You won't always be there.
So love me when I'm gone.
Love me when I'm gone.

When your education x-ray
Cannot see under my skin.
I won't tell you a damn thing
That I could not tell my friends.
Roaming through this darkness,
I'm alive but I'm alone.
And part of me is fighting this,
But part of me is gone.

Refrain

Maybe I'm just blind.

Refrain

Love me when I'm gone, when I'm gone,
When I'm gone, when I'm gone.

Where Were You (When the World Stopped Turning)

Words and Music by Alan Jackson

recorded by Alan Jackson

Where were you when the world stopped turnin'
That September day?
Out in the yard with your wife and children
Or workin' on some stage in L.A.?
Did you stand there in shock at the sight of that black smoke
Risin' against that blue sky?
Did you shout out in anger, in fear for your neighbor,
Or did you just sit down and cry?

Did you weep for the children, they lost their dear loved ones,
Pray for the ones who don't know?
Did you rejoice for the people who walked from the rubble
And sob for the ones left below?
Did you burst out in pride for the red, white, and blue
And heroes who died just doin' what they do?
Did you look up to heaven for some kind of answer
And look at yourself and what really matters?

Refrain:
I'm just a singer of simple songs.
I'm not a real political man.
I watch CNN, but I'm not sure I can tell you
The difference in Iraq and Iran.
But I know Jesus and I talk to God,
And I remember this from when I was young:
Faith, hope, and love are some good things He gave us
And the greatest is love.

Where were you when the world stopped turnin'
That September day?
Teachin' a class full of innocent children
Or drivin' on some cold interstate?
Did you feel guilty 'cause you're a survivor?
In a crowded room did you feel alone?
Did you call up your mother and tell her you love her?
Did you dust off that Bible at home?

Did you open your eyes and hope it never happened,
Close your eyes and not go to sleep?
Did you notice the sunset for the first time in ages
And speak to some stranger on the street?
Did you lay down at night and think of tomorrow,
Go out and buy you a gun?
Did you turn off that violent old movie you're watchin'
And turn on "I Love Lucy" reruns?
Did you go to a church and hold hands with some stranger,
Stand in line to give your own blood?
Did you just stay home and cling tight to your family,
Thank God you had somebody to love?

Refrain Twice

And the greatest is love,
And the greatest is love.
Where were you when the world stopped turnin'
That September day?

Wherever You Will Go

Words and Music by Aaron Kamin and Alex Band

recorded by The Calling

So lately, been wonderin
Who will be there to take my place.
When I'm gone you'll need love
To light the shadow on your face.
If a great wave shall fall and fall upon us all.
Then between the sand and stone,
Could you make it on your own?

Refrain:
If I could, then I would.
I'll go wherever you will go.
Way up high or down low,
I'll go wherever you will go.

And maybe I'll find out
A way to take it back someday
To watch you, to guide you,
Through the darkest of your days.
If a great wave shall fall and fall upon us all
Then hope there's someone out there
Who can bring me back to you.

Refrain

Run away with my heart.
Run away with my hope.
Run away with my love.
I know now, just quite how
My life and love might still go on.
In your heart, and in your mind
I'll stay with you for all of time.

Refrain

If I could turn back time,
I'll go wherever you will go.
If I could make you mine,
I'll go wherever you will go.
I'll go wherever you will go.

White Flag

Words and Music by Rick Nowels, Rollo Armstrong and Dido Armstrong

recorded by Dido

I know you think that I shouldn't still love you,
I'll tell you that.
But if I didn't say it, well, I'd still have felt it.
Where's the sense in that?
I promise I'm not trying to make your life harder;
I'll return to where we were.

Refrain:
But I will go down with this ship;
And I won't put my hands up and surrender.
There will be no white flag above my door;
I'm in love, and always will be.

I know I left too much mess and destruction
To come back again.
And I caused nothing but trouble;
I understand if you can't talk to me again.
And if you live by the rules that it's over,
Then I'm sure that that makes sense.

Refrain

And when we meet, which I'm sure we will,
All that was there will be there still.
I'll let it pass, and hold my tongue,
And you will think that I've moved on.

Refrain Three Times

Yeah!

Words and Music by James Phillips, La Marquis Jefferson, Christopher Bridges,
Jonathan Smith and Sean Garrett

recorded by Usher featuring Lil Jon & Ludacris

Spoken:
Yeah, okay. Usher, Usher, Usher,
Ah, let's go.

Sung:
Yeah, yeah, yeah, yeah, yeah, yeah.
Yeah, yeah, yeah, yeah, yeah, yeah.

Up in the club with my homies
Tryin' to get a little V.I.
Keep it down on the low key, low key,
'Cause you know how it feels.
I saw this shorty she was checkin' up on me.
From the game she was spittin' in my ear
You would think that she knew me, knew me.
I decided to chill. Conversation got heavy.
She had me feelin' like she's ready to blow.
Spoken: Watch out, watch out.
Sung: She was sayin' come get me
So I got up and followed her to the floor.
She said baby let's go.

When I told her I said yeah, yeah.
Shorty got down low and said come and get me.
Yeah, yeah, I got so caught up I forgot she told me.
Yeah, yeah, her and my girl used to be the best of homies.
Yeah, yeah, next thing I knew she was all up on me
Screamin' yeah, yeah, yeah, yeah, yeah, yeah.
Yeah, yeah, yeah, yeah, yeah, yeah.

She's all up in my head now.
Got me thinkin' that it might be a good idea
To take her with me, with me,
'Cause she's ready to leave. Ready to leave now.
But I gotta keep it real now 'cause on a one to ten
She's a certified twenty. But that just ain't me.
Hey 'cause I don't know if I take that chance
Just where's it gonna lead.
But what I do know is the way she dance
Makes shorty alright with me.
The way she get low, I'm like, yeah,
Work that out for me.
She asked for one more dance and I'm like yeah.

And I said yeah, yeah.
Shorty got down low and said come and get me.
Yeah, yeah, I got so caught up I forgot she told me.
Yeah, yeah, her and my girl used to be the best of homies.
Yeah, yeah, next thing I knew she was all up on me
Screamin' yeah, yeah, yeah, yeah, yeah, yeah.

Rap:
Watch out, my outfit's ridiculous.
In the club lookin' so conspicuous.
And wow, these women all on the prowl.
If you hold their head steady, I'm gon' milk the cow.
Just forget about game, I'm gon' spit the truth.
I won't stop 'til I get 'em in their birthday suits.
So gimme the rhythm and it'll be off with their clothes.
Then bend over to the front and touch your toes.
I left the Jag and I took the Rolls.
If they ain't cuttin' it I put 'em on foot patrol
Ow, how you like me now?
When my piggies die get over three hundred thousand.
Let's drink. You the one to please.
Ludacris fill cups like double D's
Me and Usher want more when we leaves 'em dead.
We want a lady in the street but freak in the bed that say...

Sung:
When I told her I said yeah, yeah.
Shorty got down low and said come and get me.
Yeah, yeah, I got so caught up I forgot she told me.
Yeah, yeah, her and my girl used to be the best of homies.
Yeah, yeah, next thing I knew she was all up on me
Screamin' yeah, yeah, yeah, yeah, yeah, yeah.
Yeah, yeah, yeah, yeah, yeah, yeah.

Spoken:
Take that and rewind it back.
Lil' John got the beat to make your booty go (clap).
Take that, rewind it back.
Usher got the voice to make your booty go (clap).
Take that, rewind it back.
Ludacris got the flow to make your booty go (clap).
Take that, rewind it back.
Lil' John got the beat to make your booty go (clap).

White Houses

Words and Music by Vanessa Carlton and Stephan Jenkins

recorded by Vanessa Carlton

Crashed on the floor when I moved in,
This little bungalow with some strange new friends.
Stay up too late and I'm too thin.
We promise each other it's till the end.
Now we're spinning empty bottles, it's the five of us
With pretty-eyed boys girls die to trust.
I can't resist the day. No, I can't resist the day.

And Jenny screams out and it's no pose,
'Cause when she dances she goes and goes.
And beer through the nose on an inside joke.
And I'm so excited, I haven't spoken.
And she's so pretty and she's so sure.
Maybe I'm more clever than a girl like her.
Summer's all in bloom. The summer's ending soon.

It's alright and it's nice not to be so alone
But I hold on to her secrets in white houses.

Maybe I'm a little bit over my head.
I come undone at the things he said.
And he's so funny in his bright red shirt.
We were all in love and we all got hurt.
I sneak into his car's black leather seat.
The smell of gasoline in the summer heat.
Boy, we're goin' way too fast. It's all too sweet to last.

It's alright and I put myself in his hands.
But I hold on to his secrets in white houses.

Love, or something ignites in my veins
And I pray it never fades in white houses.

My first time, hard to explain.
Rush of blood, oh, and a little bit of pain.
On a cloudy day, it's more common than you think.
He's my first mistake.
Maybe you were all faster than me.
We gave each other up so easily.
These silly little wounds will never mend.
I feel so far from where I've been.

So I go and I will not be back here again.
I'm gone as the day is fading on white houses.

I lie, put my injuries all in the dust.
In my heart is the five of us in white houses.
And you, maybe you'll remember me.
What I gave is yours to keep in white houses.
In white houses. In white houses.

Why Can't I?

Words and Music by Liz Phair, Graham Edwards, Scott Spock and Lauren Christy

recorded by Liz Phair

Get a load of me, get a load of you,
Walking down the street and I hardly know you.
It's just like we were meant to be.
Holding hands with you, and we're out at night.
Got a girlfriend; you say it isn't right.
And I've got someone waiting, too.
What if this is just the beginning?
We're already wet and we're gonna go swimming.

Refrain:
Why can't I breathe whenever I think about you?
Why can't I speak whenever I talk about you?
It's inevitable, it's a fact that we're gonna get down to it.
So tell me, why can't I breathe whenever I think about you?

Isn't this the best part of breaking up,
Finding someone else you can't get enough of,
Someone who wants to be with you, too?
It's an itch we know we are gonna scratch.
Gonna take a while for this egg to hatch,
But wouldn't it be beautiful?
Here we go, we're at the beginning.
We haven't fucked yet, but my head's spinning.

Refrain

High enough for you to make me wonder where it's going.
High enough for you to pull me under.
Somthings's growing out of this that we can't control.
Baby, I am dyin'.
Why can't I breathe whenever I think about you?
Why can't I speak whenever I talk about you?

Refrain

Whenever I think about you. Whenever I think about you.
Whenever I think about you. Whenever I think about you.

Yellow

Words and Music by Guy Berryman, Jon Buckland, Will Champion and Chris Martin

recorded by Coldplay

Look at the stars;
Look at how they shine for you,
And everything you do.
Yeah, they were all yellow.

I came along; I wrote a song for you
And all the things you do,
And it was called "Yellow."
So then I took my turn.
Oh, what a thing to have done;
And it was all yellow.

Your skin, oh yeah, your skin and bones
Turn into something beautiful.
And you know, you know I love you so,
You know I love you so.

I swam across, I jumped across for you.
Oh, what a thing to do,
'Cause you were all yellow.
I drew a line, I drew a line for you.
Oh, what a thing to do;
And they was all yellow.

Your skin, oh yeah, your skin and bones
Turn into something beautiful.
And you know, for you I bleed myself dry,
For you I bleed myself dry.

It's true; look how they shine for you,
Look how they shine for you.
Look how they shine for...

Look how they shine for you,
Look how they shine for you,
Look how they shine.

Look at the stars;
Look how they shine for you
And all the things that you do.

You Don't Know My Name

Words and Music by Alicia Keys, Kanye Omari West, Harold Spencer Lilly,
J.R. Bailey, Mel Kent and Ken Williams

recorded by Alicia Keys

Baby, baby, baby, from the day I saw you
I really, really want to catch your eye.
There's something special 'bout you.
I must really like you,
'Cause not a lot of guys are worth my time.
Ooh baby, baby, baby it's getting' kind of crazy,
'Cause you are takin' over my mind,

Refrain:
And it feels like, ooh. You don't know my name.
I swear, it feels like, ooh. You don't know my name.
'Round and 'round and 'round we go.
Will you ever know?

Baby, baby, baby, I see us on our first date,
You doin' everything to make me smile.
And when we had our first kiss,
Happened on a Thursday, and ooh,
It set my soul on fire.
Ooh, baby, baby, baby, I can't wait for the first time,
My imagination's runnin' wild.

Refrain

Spoken:
I'm sayin', he don't even know what he's doin' to me.
Got me feelin' all crazy inside. I'm feelin' like,

Sung:
Oh, ooh. I'm doin' more
Than I've ever done for anyone's attention.
Take notice of what's in front of you,
'Cause did I mention you're about to miss a good thing?
And you'll never know
How good it feels to have all of my affection,
And you'll never get a chance to experience my lovin'.

Refrain

Will you ever know it?
No, no, no, no, no, no, no.
Will you ever know it?

Spoken:
Well, I'm gonna have to just go ahead and call this boy.
Hello? Can I speak to Michael?
Oh, hey, how you doing?
Uh, I feel kind of silly doing this, but uh,
This is the waitress from the coffee house
On thirty-ninth and Lennox.
You know, the one with the braids? Yeah.
Well, I see you on Wednesdays all the time.
You come in every Wednesday on your lunch break, I think,
And you always order the special, with the hot chocolate.
My manager be trippin' and stuff,
Talkin' about, we gotta use water, but
I always use some milk and cream for you, 'cause
I think you're kind of sweet (laughs).

Anyway, you always got on some fly blue suit
And your cufflinks are shining all bright.
So, what you do? Oh work? Yeah that's interesting.
Look, man, I mean, I don't wanna waste your time,
But, I know girls don't usually do this,
But I was wondering if maybe we could get together
Outside the restaurant one day?
You know, 'cause I do look a lot different
Outside my work clothes, and, I mean, we could just go
Across the street to the park, right here.
Wait, hold up. My cell phone's breaking up.
Hold up, Can you hear me now?
Yeah, so what day did you say?
Oh yeah, Thursday's perfect, man.

Sung:
Baby I swear, it's like, ooh. You don't know my name.
'Round and 'round we go. Will you ever know?
And it feels like, ooh. You don't know my name.
'Round and 'round and 'round we go.
And I swear on my mother and father,
It feels like, ooh, ooh, you don't know my name.
'Round and 'round and 'round we go.
Will you ever know?

You Raise Me Up

Words and Music by Brendan Graham and Rolf Lovland

recorded by Josh Groban

When I am down and oh, my soul's so weary,
When troubles come and my heart burdened be,
Then I am still and wait here in the silence
Until you come and sit awhile with me.

Refrain Four Times:
You raise me up so I can stand on mountains.
You raise me up to walk on stormy seas.
I am strong when I am on your shoulders.
You raise me up to more than I can be.

You raise me up to more than I can be.

You Rock My World

Words and Music by Rodney Jerkins, LaShawn Daniels, Fred Jerkins III,
Michael Jackson and Nora Payne

recorded by Michael Jackson

My life will never be the same
'Cause girl you came and changed
The way I walk, the way I talk.
I cannot explain these things I feel for you.
But girl, you know it's true.
Stay with me, fulfill my dreams
And I'll be all you need.

Oh, ooh, feels so right.
I've searched for the perfect love all my life.
Oh, ooh, feels like I have finally found
A perfect love this time.
I've finally found, so come on, girl.

Refrain (Sing Twice):
You rocked my work, you know you did,
And everything I own I give.
The rarest love, who'd think I'd find
Someone like you to call mine?

In time I knew that love would bring
Such happiness to me.
I tried to keep my sanity; I've waited patiently.
Girl know it seems my life is so complete.
A love that's true because of you.
Keep doin' what you do.

Oh, ooh. Think that I've finally found
The perfect love I've searched for all my life.
Oh, who'd think I'd find such a perfect love
That's awesomely so right.

Refrain Twice

Girl, I know that this is love.
I felt the magic's all in the air.
And girl, I'll never get enough,
That a-why I always have to have you here.

Refrain Twice

You rock my world.
(You rocked my world you know you did.)
The way you talk to me, the way you're lovin' me,
You, the way you give it to me.
(You rocked my world, you know you did.)
Give it to me. Yeah, yeah, you, you, yeah, yeah.

You rock my world. You rock my world.
(You rocked my world, you know you did.)
You rock my world. You rock my world.
You rock my world. You rock my world.
Come on girl.

Refrain Twice

You Sang to Me

Words and Music by Cory Rooney and Marc Anthony

recorded by Marc Anthony

I just wanted you to comfort me
When I called you late last night.
You see, I was falling into love,
Yes, I was crashing into love.
Oh, of all the words you said to me
About life, the truth, and being free, yeah,
You sang to me, oh, how you sang to me.

Girl, I live for how you make me feel,
So I question all this being real,
'Cause I'm not afraid to love;
For the first time I'm not afraid of love.
Oh, this day seems made for you and me
And you showed me what life needs to be.
Yeah, you sang to me, oh, you sang to me.

Refrain:
All the while you were in front of me I never realized.
I just can't believe I didn't see it in your eyes.
I didn't see it, I can't believe it.
Oh, but I feel it when you sing to me.
How I long to hear you sing beneath the clear blue skies,
And I promise you this time I'll see it in your eyes.
I didn't see it, I can't believe it,
Oh, but I feel it when you sing to me.

Just to think you live inside of me.
I had no idea how this could be.
Now I'm crazy for your love.
Can't believe I'm crazy for your love.
The words you said just sang to me
And you showed me where I wanna be.
You sang to me, oh, you sang to me.